Franka Grünewald

Uniting the Social Web and Topic Maps with Tele-Teaching to Provide User-Friendly Interaction Possibilities with E-Lectures

Die vorliegende Arbeit wurde im Juli 2014 von der mathematisch-naturwissenschaftlichen Fakultät an der Universität Potsdam als Dissertation zur Erlangung des akademischen Grades Doktor der Naturwissenschaften (Dr. rer. nat.) angenommen.

1. Gutachter: Prof. Dr. Christoph Meinel
                     Hasso-Plattner-Institut

2. Gutachter: Prof. Dr.-Ing. habil. Ulrike Lucke
                     Universität Potsdam

3. Gutachter: Prof. Matjaz Debevc
                     Universität Maribor

Bibliografische Informationen der Deutschen Nationalbibliothek
Die Deutsche Nationalbibliothek verzeichnet diese Publikation in der Deutschen Nationalbibliografie; detaillierte bibliografische Daten sind im Internet über http://dnb.d-nb.de abrufbar.

ISBN 978-3-8325-3792-0

Logos Verlag Berlin GmbH
Comeniushof, Gubener Str. 45
10243 Berlin
Tel.: +49 (0)30 42 85 10 90
Fax: +49 (0)30 42 85 10 92

This work is dedicated to my husband and my parents.

Danksagung

Die vorliegende Arbeit entstand während meiner Zeit als Doktorandin am Lehrstuhl für Internet-Technologien und -Systeme des Hasso-Plattner-Instituts. Sie fußt auf den Projekten tele-TASK und openHPI, ohne deren Grundlagen diese Arbeit nicht möglich gewesen wäre. Hiermit möchte ich meinem Betreuer und Doktorvater, Prof. Dr. Christoph Meinel, dafür danken, dass er mir die Möglichkeit gab an seinem Lehrstuhl in vielseitigen Projekten und Verantwortlichkeiten arbeiten und mich weiterentwickeln zu können und es mir durch die Konferenzteilnahmen und Weiterbildungen ermöglichte, den Blick über den Tellerrand hinaus zu werfen.

Bei meinen Gutachtern Prof. Ulrike Lucke und Prof. Matjaz Debevc möchte ich mich für das intensive Feedback und die Diskussionen über meine Arbeit bedanken. Prof. Lucke hat mir durch ihre Vorbildfunktion auch gezeigt, dass die Vereinbarkeit von Familie und einer Arbeit in der Wissenschaft praktisch realisierbar ist und mich fortwährend ermutigt, diesen Weg weiter zu gehen und diese Arbeit abzuschließen, wofür ich ihr ebenfalls sehr danke.

Ganz besonders möchte ich mich auch bei meinen Kollegen und Freunden Maria Siebert, Haojin Yang, Raja Gumienny und Michael Totschnig, sowie vielen weiteren bedanken, die mich in diesen Jahren begleitet, und in zahlreichen Diskussionen und Gesprächen inspiriert und fachlich unterstützt haben. Gerda Siebert, Julia von Thienen und Franziska Göbel danke ich für die Diskussionen über Statistik. Meinem Bruder Stefan und Bettina Kreuzburg bin ich für die umfassenden Englischkorrekturen zu großem Dank verpflichtet.

Mein besonderer Dank gilt auch Florian Moritz, Alexander Schulze, Lukas Schulze und Kai Fabian, die als studentische Mitarbeiter die Implementierung des tele-TASK Portals, insbesondere der in dieser Arbeit vorgestellten Nutzerfunktionen, tatkräftig unterstützt haben. Allen Experten und Probanden danke ich für Ihre Mitarbeit und Rückmeldungen für die Evaluationen.

Mein tiefster Dank gilt meiner Familie. Bei meinen Eltern bedanke ich mich für die kontinuierliche Ermutigung, den fortwährenden Glauben an mich und die Unterstützung, die mir sowohl das Studium als auch die Promotion ermöglichten. Meinem Mann Norbert danke ich für seine Liebe und dafür, dass er stets die Ruhe bewahrt, mich ermutigt und durch großen Einsatz seinerseits den Rücken für die Dissertation freigehalten hat. Bei meiner Tochter Johanna bedanke ich mich für ihr Verständnis, dass Mama lange wenig Zeit hatte. Beiden Kindern, Johanna und Jonathan, danke ich für die wunderbaren Momente, die sie täglich in unser Leben bringen.

Zusammenfassung

Vorlesungsaufzeichnungen, so genannte E-Lectures, sind heutzutage an den Universitäten sehr verbreitet. Dennoch gibt es in diesem Zusammenhang zwei Probleme. Zum einen ist es für die Nutzer sehr einfach, sich passiv zu verhalten, was aus lerntheoretischer Sicht ausgesprochen ungünstig ist. Zum anderen ist das Finden relevanter Inhalte durch die Menge an Vorlesungsaufzeichnung bei gleichzeitig mangelnder Metadatenbasis eine Herausforderung.

Aufgrund dieser beiden Problematiken beschäftigt sich diese Dissertation mit dem Einsatz von Technologien des Web 2.0 und des Semantic Web zur Bereitstellung von Interaktionmöglichkeiten mit Vorlesungsaufzeichnungen. Der Sinn der mit Hilfe des Web 2.0 und dem Semantic Web entwickelten Werkzeuge, ist die Aktivierung der Nutzer und die Unterstützung des Suchprozesses nach Lerninhalten. Die Studierenden, die die E-Lectures sehen, sollen in die Lage versetzt werden, aktiv mit den Materialien zu arbeiten, kollaborativ Lerninhalte zu erstellen und selbständig Themengebiete zu erschließen.

Zunächst wurden diverse Nutzerfunktionen wie Tagging, Bewertungen und Playlisten umgesetzt, um die Studierenden zu aktivieren. Dennoch war festzustellen, dass die Anwenderaktivität sehr gering war. Als Gründe dafür wurden zu wenig Anreiz zur Partizipation und unzureichender zusätzlicher Nutzen der Funktionen außerhalb der Aktivität identifiziert. Eine kollaborative Annotations-Umgebung mit partizipativen Elementen ist als eine Lösung für die mangelnde Beteiligung implementiert und evaluiert worden.

Darüberhinaus wurde die Möglichkeit untersucht, weitere Vorteile aus der Annotationen für die Studierenden zu generieren, um erwähntem Grundproblem des Findens relevanter Inhalte zu begegnen. Eine semantische Topic Map wurde dazu als Ergänzung zu dem Annotationswerkzeug entwickelt. Mit Hilfe des Semantik Web können zu Begriffen innerhalb der nutzer-generierten Annotation Topic Maps verknüpft werden, die den Kontext dieses Wortes darstellen und geeignete Lernvideos aufzeigen. Die Evaluation erfolgte durch Expertenbewertung und Nutzertests.

Abstract

Lecture recordings, so called e-lectures, are widely spread across universities. But, concerning those e-lectures, there exist two problems. On the one hand, it is very easy for users just to lean back and not become active. From the perspective of learning theory, this is no desirable state. On the other hand, it is a challenge to find relevant content from the mass of lecture recordings when at the same time there is not a sufficient amount of metadata available.

Due to these two issues, this dissertation deals with the utilization of Web 2.0 and Semantic Web technologies to provide interaction possibilities with e-lectures. The aim of the tools developed in this work with the help of Web 2.0 and Semantic Web technologies is to activate users and support the search process for learning content. The students watching the e-lectures should be able to actively work with learning material, collaboratively acquire new learning content and independently identify new topic areas.

Initially, many user functions like tagging, rating and playlists were implemented in order to activate the participants. However, user activity was still low. Reasons identified were for example little incentive for participation and little added value of the function beyond the activity. A collaborative annotation environment with participative elements was implemented and evaluated as one solution for the participation problem.

Furthermore, the possibility to generate added value for students was researched. Since finding the relevant content is another major issue, the added value was to tackle this problem. A semantic topic map was implemented as an extension to the lecture video annotation function. With the help of methods from the Semantic Web, keywords within the user-generated annotation can be linked to topic maps. These topic maps visualize the context of the keywords and indicate appropriate learning videos.

The evaluation of the annotation functions and the topic map was conducted by expert review and user tests.

Contents

CONTENTS

List of Publications by the Author

[1] Franka Grünewald, Haojin Yang, and Christoph Meinel. Evaluating the Digital Manuscript Functionality - User Testing For Lecture Video Annotation Features. In *ICWL 2013 - 12th International Conference on Web-based Learning*, Kenting, Taiwan, 2013. best student paper award. 57, 91, 92

[2] Haojin Yang, Franka Grünewald, Matthias Bauer, and Christoph Meinel. Lecture Video Browsing Using Multimodal Information Resources. In *ICWL 2013 - 12th International Conference on Web-based Learning*, Kenting, Taiwan, 2013. 35, 91, 92, 95

[3] Franka Grünewald and Christoph Meinel. Social Semantic Keywords - Finding a Way to Enhance User-generated Metadata in Tele-Teaching - Poster Paper. In *Gracehopper Celebration of Women in Computing*, Minneapolis, USA, 2013. 34, 35

[4] Franka Grünewald and Christoph Meinel. Female Participation in MOOCs - Do Women Learn Differently in Computer Science Courses? - Poster Paper. In *Gracehopper Celebration of Women in Computing*, Minneapolis, USA, 2013.

[5] Franka Grünewald, Christoph Meinel, Michael Totschnig, and Christian Willems. Designing MOOCs for the Support of Multiple Learning Styles. In *EC-TEL 2013 - Eigth European Conference on Technology Enhanced Learning*, Paphos, Cyprus, 2013. Springer. 19, 20, 21, 22, 23, 26, 92

[6] Franka Grünewald, Elnaz Mazandarani, Christoph Meinel, Ralf Teusner, Michael Totschnig, and Christian Willems. openHPI: Soziales und Praktisches Lernen im Kontext eines MOOC. In *DeLFI 2013 - Deutsche E-Learning Fachtagung der Gesellschaft für Informatik*, 2013. 19, 22, 23, 92

[7] Franka Grünewald, Haojin Yang, Elnaz Mazandarani, Matthias Bauer, and Christoph Meinel. Next Generation Tele-Teaching: Latest Recording Technology, User Engagement and Automatic Metadata Retrieval. In *SouthCHI 2013 - International Conference on Human Factors in Computing & Informatics*, Maribor, Slovenia, 2013. Springer. 11, 13, 16, 57

[8] Franka Grünewald, Elnaz Mazandarani, Christoph Meinel, Ralf Teusner, Michael Totschnig, and Christian Willems. openHPI - a Case-Study on the Emergence of two Learning Communities. In *EDUCON 2013 - IEEE Global Engineering Education Conference*, 2013. 1, 3, 4, 19, 92

[9] Franka Grünewald and Christoph Meinel. Implementing a Culture of Participation as Means for Collaboration in Tele-Teaching Using the Example of Cooperative Video Annotation. In *DeLFI 2012 - Die 10. e-Learning Fachtagung Informatik*, Hagen, Germany, 2012. Gesellschaft für Informatik. 16, 24, 25, 27, 28, 29, 57

[10] Franka Grünewald, Maria Siebert, Alexander Schulze, and Christoph Meinel. Automatic Categorization of Lecture Videos: Using Statistical Log File Analysis To Enhance Tele-Teaching Metadata. In *DeLFI 2012 - Die 10. e-Learning Fachtagung Informatik*, Hagen, Germany, 2012. Gesellschaft für Informatik. 41

[11] Haojin Yang, Franka Grünewald, and Christoph Meinel. Automated Extraction of Lecture Outlines From Lecture Videos - A Hybrid Solution for Lecture Video Indexing. In *4th International Conference on Computer Supported Education*, pages 13–22, Porto, Portugal, 2012. 4, 35, 92

[12] Franka Gruenewald, Maria Siebert, and Christoph Meinel. Leveraging Social Web Functionalities in Tele-Teaching Platforms. *International Journal for Digital Society*, 2(3), 2011. 16, 27, 56

[13] Franka Moritz, Maria Siebert, and Christoph Meinel. Improving Search in Tele-Lecturing: Using Folksonomies as Trigger to Query Semantic Datasets to extract additional metadata. In *Proceedings of the International Conference on Web Intelligence, Mining and Semantics - WIMS '11*, New York, New York, USA, May 2011. ACM Press. 34, 35, 42, 70, 71

[14] Franka Moritz, Maria Siebert, and Christoph Meinel. Community Tagging in Tele-Teaching Environments. In *2nd International Conference on e-Education, e-Business, e-Management and E-Learning*, Mumbai, India, 2011. 17, 27, 52, 53, 55

[15] Maria Siebert, Franka Moritz, and Christoph Meinel. Report on the Project : Enlargement of the Search Domain of the tele-TASK Portal. Technical report, Universitätsverlag Potsdam, Potsdam, 2011.

[16] Maria Siebert, Franka Moritz, Frank Hambach, and Christoph Meinel. Enriching E-Learning meta data with user generated playlists. In *5th International Conference for Internet Technology and Secured Transactions*, London, UK, 2010. IEEE Press. 27, 55

[17] Franka Moritz, Maria Siebert, and Christoph Meinel. Improving Community Rating in the Tele-Lecturing Context. In *5th International Conference for Internet Technology and Secured Transactions*, London, UK, 2010. IEEE Press. 17, 27, 51

[18] Franka Moritz, Maria Siebert, and Christoph Meinel. Community Rating in the Tele-Lecturing Context. In *IAENG International Conference on Internet Computing and Web Services (ICICWS'10)*, Hong Kong, 2010. IAENG. 17, 27, 51

[19] Maria Siebert, Franka Moritz, and Christoph Meinel. Distributed Recognition of Content Similarity in a Tele-Teaching Portal. In *2nd International Conference on Information and Multimedia Technology (ICIMT 2010)*, Hong-Kong, 2010. 53

[20] Maria Siebert, Franka Moritz, and Christoph Meinel. Establishing an Expandable Architecture for a tele-Teaching Platform. In *Ninth IEEE/ACIS International Conference on Computer and Information Science*, Yamagata, Japan, 2010. IEEE Press. 14

[21] Andreas Groß, Christoph Meinel, Franka Moritz, and Maria Siebert. Aufbau eines Multi-Plattform-Lernvideo-Archivs: Herausforderungen und Lösungen. In Andreas Hohenstein and Prof. Dr. Karl Wilbers, editors, *Handbuch E-Learning*. Wolters & Kluwer, 2010. 50

[22] Franka Moritz and Christoph Meinel. Mobile Web Usability Evaluation - Combining the Modified Think Aloud Method with the Testing of Emotional , Cognitive and Conative Aspects of the Usage of a Web Application. In *Ninth IEEE/ACIS International Conference on Computer and Information Science*, Yamagata, Japan, 2010. IEEE Press.

[23] Franka Moritz. Potentials of 3D-Web-Applications in E-Commerce - Study about the Impact of 3D-Product-Presentations. In *Ninth IEEE/ACIS International Conference on Computer and Information Science*, Yamagata, Japan, 2010. IEEE Press.

LIST OF PUBLICATIONS BY THE AUTHOR

List of Figures

List of Tables

LIST OF TABLES

Listings

LISTINGS

Chapter 1

Introduction

Online and distance learning are the fastest growing areas of educational development in the world (Sim13). In autumn 2011, 6.7 million students were enrolled in at least one online course in the United States alone (AS13). This means that in total more than 32% of the higher education students took at least one online course. This trend is also reflected in the mindset of academic leaders. 69.1% of U.S. scientific senior executives confirm that e-learning is a critical matter in their long-term strategy (AS13). Considering the importance of e-learning for higher education, institutions interested in applying it, need to question themselves about the success factors for the digital education. These criteria for success (LS12) are:

- Simplification for lecturers needs to be achieved.

- Added value and quality of experience for learners should be provided.

- In parallel, a cultural change has to happen in the educational institutions.

Online education is a means to reach more people, save money and offer multimedia experiences. The quality of studying with e-learning tools is in discussion, though. On the one hand, didacts argue that already using the systems places enormous demands on the individual's learning competences and e-learning has thus not been able to meet the expectations, yet (Sch07, Ehl11). On the other hand, for instance 77% of U.S. academic leaders consider the learning outcomes in e-learning the same as or even superior to those in a face-to-face setting with a rising trend (AS13).

Despite the benefits and the success stories, which have just recently been complemented by the rise of Massive Open Online Courses (Rod12, Sie12, GMM$^+$13a, CM14), there are many research challenges in e-learning remaining (DHK$^+$11, LS12, KW12). A major challenge is the interdisciplinary nature of e-learning (KW12). Already looking at the word e-learning, one can see that on the one side the *e* reflects the use of some kind of technological baseline that requires computer science knowledge, whereas on the other side the *learning* part demands didactical knowledge. Several researchers (Bau10, LS12) identified the specialized didactics of the disciplines as well as psychology as further disciplines involved. Looking at validating research findings in the field of e-learning, methods from social sciences are often applied as well.

In this work, the goal is not to see the interdisciplinary nature of e-learning as a challenge, but as an opportunity for research. When combining literature and methods from all previously mentioned areas, the challenges will be tackled from all different perspectives. Figure 1.1 shows an overview of the problem areas involved in e-learning research and production and depicts the research process applied in this work by visualizing which discipline is tangented to which research phase.

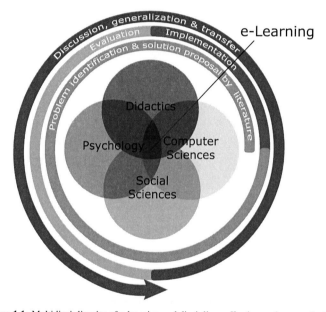

Figure 1.1: Multidisciplinarity of e-learning and disciplines affecting each research phase

E-learning is situated at the intersection of didactics, computer sciences, social sciences and psychology. The *research spiral* starts from the inside with problem identification and solution proposal, which includes literature from each of the four perspectives. The next step is the implementation of prototypes. Methods from computer science are used for the development of technical prototypes, which are implemented for specific didactical scenarios. IT problems are exposed and solved in this phase. Later on in the evaluation, the tools are employed in didactical scenarios. Techniques from empirical social research and psychology are applied to conduct the evaluations. User testing methods (like for example the Think-Aloud-Method) and interviews are often employed to analyze technical prototypes with users on a qualitative basis. Questionnaires and quizzes together with a statistical evaluation are frequently utilized for quantitative evaluations. In order to interpret the results, the interdisciplinary findings will be analysed and discussed together with literature from all the disciplines.

Research findings support the presumption that video recordings of lectures, so-called e-lectures, play a key role in online education (VAG[+]11). Looking at the success factors for online education, the simplification for the lecturers is definitely a pro argument for tele-teaching since it is relatively easy, cheap, scalable as well as time independent. A cultural change in the institutions can also be noticed. Because lecture recording systems (like tele-TASK[1] (SM02), Camtasia Studio[2] or Lecturnity[3]) are becoming faster and easier to use, the number of educational video data grows rapidly. Thousands of lecture videos may even be available for a small institute (GMM[+]13a). These are also the basis for the recently emerged and very popular e-learning format of Massive Open Online Courses (MOOC), specifically the xMOOC format. XMOOCs were initially made known by the Stanford University in the United States (Sie12). From the learner's perspective, the added value can be understood in terms of learning independent from time and place. The quality of the learning experience is questionable, though.

With the number of available resources growing, new challenges arise for the learners nowadays. They only have limited time to run through these resources and find the information they are looking for. Searching through the whole video for a very specific or even unspecific information or quickly getting an overview of a lecture video's content, are major issues for the students (ZH02, Hür03, WLKS11). The reason is, that searching through videos is not trivial due to the nature of videos (Her11b). Videos are multimedia content, they cannot easily be indexed or searched. Until now, administrative metadata has been a popular solution to search and filtering issues by institutions being responsible for the content provisioning (KSH10).

Two paths to the solution of this problem can be envisioned. Automatic metadata harvesting is the first one (EMC03, GKK05, FW08, Her11b, Yan13). The basis for metadata extraction are the audio data from the lecturer's speech as well as the image data from the video. Optical character recognition (OCR) (FW08) and audio transcription (ASR) (EMC03, Yan13) technologies are established to extract textual data from the video. In order to render the withdrawn material usable, finding the essential in-

[1] www.tele-task.de
[2] www.techsmith.de/camtasia.html
[3] www.lecturnity.de

3

formation within the large amount of unprioritized data is the next challenge. Video indexing tools, like a lecture structure, gathered from the lecturer's slide and enhanced with direct links into the video (YGM12), automatically extracted slides in a timeline format as well as a keyword searching tool (GMM+13a) can support reaching this purpose.

The second path grew with the beginning of the Web 2.0 (Rei07). With the Web 2.0, Tim O'Reilly introduced the idea of online communities where users are responsible for creating and sharing their own web content. The main advantages of Web 2.0 principles for tele-teaching are the idea of collaborating in communities, active engagement and large amounts of metadata being created by the users. From the didactical point of view, the collaboration with fellow students and the active commitment with the learning content are major benefits. This is even more true for e-lectures. In order to be attentive for 90 minutes of a lecture while being on their own at home in front of the computer, students need a lot of self-discipline. Research proved that in distance learning especially the exchange with other learners and the active involvement with the material are of major importance. There are numerous Web 2.0 functions available. The contexts in which they should be used for studying have not yet been researched in a structured manner, though (DHK+11). Also, the technical requirements for an effective use of Web 2.0 tools in learning scenarios are rather unclear (DHK+11).

1.1 Problem Statement and Approaches

This thesis aims at providing tools and strategies fostering the active engagement as well as collaboration in tele-teaching and establishing mechanisms to improve searching and filtering for self-directed learning. In order to reflect on the usage of Web 2.0 tools in connection with e-lectures, several Web 2.0 functions were implemented and studied. Learners using tele-teaching are diverse. One of the criteria they vary in are their divergent learning styles. Pure video lectures will not address all the types of learners existing. In result, this work will also deliver an overview of the existing learning types and promising ways to support these.

The following key questions are answered in this dissertation:

- Do students use classic Web 2.0 features in connection with e-lectures?

- How may collaboration be fostered in a tele-teaching scenario?

- Which functions and processes need to be offered to support learners of all different learning styles when using e-lectures?

- How might students be supported in self-organized learning and search with e-lectures?

- Can research findings in tele-teaching environments be transferred to MOOC settings?

Since tele-teaching encourages the utilization of video lectures independent from time and place, it is a good medium in terms of self-directed learning. Therefore, tools and methods supporting that in conjunction e-lectures are also within the scope of this work. Finally, the latest accomplishment in e-learning, the MOOCs are addressed. By also evaluating tools developed for a university tele-teaching scenario in a MOOC setting, the approaches will be generalized.

1.2 Thesis Contributions and Dissociation

For answering the questions defined, this thesis provides multiple contributions:

- A summary of the pedagogical, psychological, sociological and information technology background to the use of e-lectures.

- An outline of learning styles according to Kolb and a mapping of tools in a MOOC scenario to support them.

- An overview of design principles to support cultures of participation transferred to tele-teaching research.

- The implementation and a short evaluation of basic Web 2.0 tools for a higher education tele-teaching setting.

- The identification and discussion of collaborative digital e-lecture annotation as a key function to facilitate engagement and cooperation.

- The implementation and evaluation of a collaborative lecture video annotation tool. The analysis compares analogue to digital (in the form of annotations), individual to collaborative and synchronous to asynchronous manuscript writing to a lecture.

- The evaluation of the digital e-lecture annotation concept in a MOOC context.

- The identification and discussion of topic maps as a way to support different learning styles as well as search and navigation for self-organized learning.

- An algorithm to automatically generate topic maps out of user-generated annotations as well as an expert evaluation of the algorithm.

- Evaluations of the topic map concept via a user-test in both, a university and a MOOC setting.

5

This theses does not aim at

- creating new interventions or teaching scenarios, where the tools developed could be utilized. The testing of the functions was conducted within known teaching constellations.

- developing new algorithms for semantic information retrieval. The algorithm introduced for the retrieval of the data used in the semantic topic map is comprised of existing algorithms that were adapted to the purpose of semantic context acquisition out of user-generated annotations.

- addressing scalability of the implemented tools.

1.3   Thesis Organization

The following roadmap visualizes the path taken to approach the questions determined for this dissertation and thus gives an overview of the research conducted within the scope of this thesis:

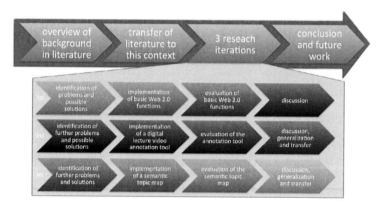

Figure 1.2: Roadmap of the PhD thesis

The research started with an intense overview of the literature in related fields. The insights available were then transferred to the context of tele-teaching. Afterwards, three research iterations were passed through: problem as well as solution identification followed by implementation, evaluation and discussion including generalization.

Finally, conclusions were drawn and future work was outlined. The research was conducted following the roadmap (fig. 1.2) horizontally. In this thesis the work is presented vertically, though.

This thesis is divided into three main chapters. In the chapter *Current State of Research and Theoretical Advancements*, the technological, didactical, as well as psychological and sociological background will be elaborated. In particular, the literature basis for the implementations in this thesis will be explained and related work introduced. In the third chapter *Implementation of User-Centered Tele-Teaching Tools*, the implementation of basic Web 2.0 functions, a collaborative lecture annotation function as well as a semantic topic map in the tele-teaching context will be explained. In chapter *Evaluation*, the annotation functions, the topic map tool and the semantic context extraction algorithm providing input data for the topic map will be studied. User tests, expert reviews and questionnaires were used for the evaluation.

1. INTRODUCTION

Chapter 2

Current State of Research and Theoretical Advancements

E-Learning is "making connections among persons and resources through communication technologies (television/ video-based and computer-based) for learning-related purposes" (Col96, p. 16). E-learning environments enable individual learners to address their specific needs and interests, deepen their understanding and study several levels of complexity (Han97). Because the usage of technology brings flexibility into the learning process, the learning and thinking procedures are enriched by e-learning (HL97).

The term e-Learning has developed since about 1999. It describes a form of learning which includes the latest information and communication technologies, like computers and the internet, into learning settings (Ehl11). The technology might either be used to support learning processes or as single form of knowledge transfer (Ehl11). The utilization of digital technology for supporting learning procedures of people has had many names in history (CRH$^+$06, Ehl11). The naming started in 1989 (Ehl11) with Computer Based Instruction (CBI) (LS89), continued with Computer Based Training (CBT) (Bre90) and Computer Aided Instruction (CAI) (Bod90) in 1990, and was complimented by Computer Based Learning (CBL) (Ham93) in 1993 and Computer Aided Teaching (CAT) (GS11) as well as Computer Aided Learning (CAL) (GS11) in 1997. Interestingly, the nomenclature e-Learning denotes a digital learning process. But the learning activity itself is cannot be digital, only the intervention can be (Ehl11). Other terms in this context are educational technology, educational computing, information and communication technology in education (CRH$^+$06). In this work we use e-Learning as the term for human learning assisted by digital technology. Networked forms of e-Learning are called online learning, (open) distance learning, virtual classroom, tele-learning as well as tele-teaching (Ehl11) and networked learning (CRH$^+$06).

Those terms describe a learning setting where the teacher and the learner(s) are distant from each other (Ehl11). This separation may be spatial or temporal. Another e-Learning categorization refers to the temporal situation. It distinguishes e-Learning in synchronous (tutor and students may communicate among each other at the same time, for example via chats or video conferencing systems) and asynchronous modes (tutor and students are not present at the same time slot, but have a delayed communication or information transfer) (SJG02, Ehl11). One may also distinguish e-Learning in online as well as computer supported offline learning forms (Ehl11). The classification scheme of Bodendorf differentiates e-learning systems according to their intended purpose, like for example simulations, tutor systems etc. (Bod90). He also suggest a categorization by development tools on the one and application tools for the learners on the other side.

Dependent on if an e-learning concept is targeted at sole self study or includes a distant tutor, one differentiates between tele-learning and tele-teaching (Ueb96, Ehl11). Tele-tutoring or tele-coaching are phrases used when a distant tutor is involved and no whole classes transmitted, but the tutor is rather sporadically questioned about single problems. The term tele-learning is thus rather targeted at asynchronous learning, whereas tele-teaching is the word mostly used in the context of synchronous transmission of courses via video conferencing or video streaming (Wil94, Mil97, Aus99, Ehl11).

In this work the term tele-teaching refers to online e-learning using lecture recordings, so-called e-lectures. In contrast to the presented definitions, tele-teaching here relates to synchronous as well as asynchronous modes of working with e-lectures. The learning arrangement focuses on the transmission of lectures to a remote audience. Tele-teaching mimics classical lectures at universities (Ehl11). The learners have a receptive passive role receiving information. Communication amongst the participants is often not envisaged. User activation and engagement in tele-teaching is a field of research and development that recently emerged. It will be addressed in the remainder of this chapter.

Today's tele-teaching has several foundations and basic technology to deal with. First of all in order to produce e-lectures, lecture recording technology has to be used. Therefore the first section of this chapter will deal with current recording technology and give an overview of the state of the art. Afterwards, lecture distribution platforms are briefly summarized. The sample tele-teaching portal used as basis for the implementation and part of the research presented in this work is introduced. In order to be successful, these platforms need to be designed according to the needs of the users. According to up-to-date pedagogy user engagement is required. How a current tele-teaching platform can be designed in a user-centred manner and how it manages to engage users, will be elaborated next. Metadata is the key to success when it comes to search and filtering processes in e-lectures. Therefore, this necessary topic is addressed thereafter. One application of metadata for the sake of search and filtering processes are topic maps. Their scope and background is explained thereafter. After the theoretical part, related work will be introduced. Finally this chapter concludes by summarizing the main challenges and introducing the approaches taken in this work.

2.1   Lecture Recording Technology

Lecture recording technology enables the digitization of a lecture. In order to have a complete workflow of lecture recording and usage, recording hard- and software is used to create the so-called e-lectures. Afterwards, e-lecture distribution platforms are used to disseminate these recordings amongst the students. Therefore, this chapter will start with an overview of lecture recording hard- and software, continue with reflections on e-lecture distribution platforms before finishing with an introduction to the sample tele-teaching project this work is built upon.

2.1.1   Lecture Recording Hard- and Software

A lecture recording is composed of several signals, including the presentation the lecturer is showing, optionally a video of the lecturer talking and the audio of the speech the lecturer is giving. All those signals are fed into a lecture recording system and recorded simultaneously (see figure 2.1 for the setup with the lecture recording system tele-TASK, which will be introduced later in this section).

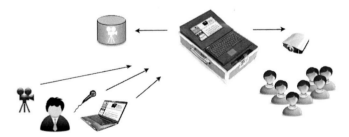

Figure 2.1: Setup required for lecture recording (GYM[+]13a).

In 1986 experiments with this kind of lecture recording systems have started at the Open University (Mas00, Her11b). In 1995 the system Authoring on the Fly (AOF), later called Lecturnity, was introduced as first tool allowing the live transmission of a digital version of a lecture to another place (OB95, Her11b). The usage of electronic boards was the next milestone in lecture recording. Electronic boards are interactive white boards, which are able to show for example presentation slides in an interactive mode and thus allow editing its content. At the Georgia Institute of Technology a lecture was made accessible electronically using an electronic board with a pen and the internet (AAF$^+$96, Her11b). In 2002 a large number of lecture recording systems including tele-TASK (SM02), Camtasia Studio [1] and virtPresenter (MKV04) were introduced to the market. For a more detailed history of lecture recording systems see the dissertation of Christoph Hermann (Her11b).

There are five different methods to record lectures on the market that are utilizing the principle of rapid authoring (Her11b). Those are object based techniques, screen-grabbing procedures, external principles as well as blackboard digitization by photographing or by using digital blackboards. Other methods include simple video recording and more advanced methods that need more authoring and post-production time. Object-based methods save the lecture objects, like the lecture slides, on a vector basis. AOF is one example of this method (OB95, Her11b). Because the objects used for the lecture remain in their original form, scaling and searching are quite easy. But a disadvantage is that this method does not allow to record everything happening in a lecture.

These disadvantages are alleviated when using the screen-grabbing procedures, like Camtasia Studio[2] or Adobe Captivate[3]. Everything happening on the screen on the presenter's laptop is thereby captured in a video. The disadvantages are that large amounts of data are produced. Both of these methods have the disadvantage to require additional software on the presenter's laptop. External methods, like those used by the tele-TASK system (SM02), capture the output of the laptop (usually via VGA), which can be done without interfering with the presenter's laptop. The last two approaches have the disadvantage, that search and filtering as well as quick skipping through the content is not so easy, because the recording is stored in a video. Further processing, like OCR and ASR analysis, or other metadata production methods are required to overcome this issue. The metadata production is further discussed in section 2.3.

2.1.2 E-Lecture Distribution Platforms

After having used lecture recording hard- and software, the lecture recording workflow continues with the post-production process and the distribution (see figure 2.2). While lecture recording hard- and software can be used to digitize a lecture, it is at the same time also possible to use a live streaming option in order to broadcast the data recorded live either into another lecture hall or to the internet. A streaming sever will be used for this option.

---

[1]http://www.techsmith.com/camtasia-version-history.html
[2]http://www.techsmith.de/camtasia.asp
[3]http://www.adobe.com/de/products/captivate/

After recording, the post-production takes place, where the videos are edited and optionally converted to different video formats, like a podcast format (WLM07). This is also the time when metadata is generated. As metadata is an important topic in the e-lecture life-cycle, it will be specifically addressed in section 2.3. After they have been processed, the videos will be stored either directly on an external medium like a CD, DVD or USB drive or in a learning video archive. This archive usually consists of a media server with streaming capability that hosts the media files and a database that stores the matching metadata. From there the video data can be distributed either via an in-house web portal, via external providers, like iTunes University (iTunes U) or YouTube (GBBM09). RSS-feeds can furthermore be used to publish the metadata and thus provide further options to access the content.

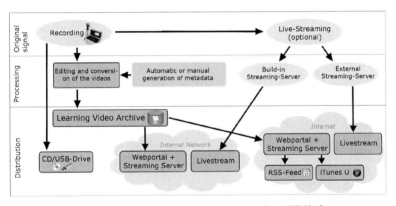

Figure 2.2: Workflow of the lecture video production (GYM$^+$13a).

Tele-teaching portals have been developed just shortly after the invention of lecture recording systems. In 1999 the Synchronized Hypermedia Live Lecture System (SHLL) is introduced, which allows the synchronization of different media streams in a browser using the Real Time Protocol (RTP) (CC96, Her11b). In the same year the Berkeley Internet Broadcasting System is introduced that even allows browsing within lectures and searching in whole lecture archives (RHPL01, Her11b). In 2001 the Massacusetts Institute of Technology (MIT) announced the start of the OpenCourseWare Project and distributed the first 50 courses to the public one year later via its tele-teaching web portal [1]. From 2003 onward e-lecture distribution platforms, like the

---

[1] http://watch.mit.edu/

13

tele-TASK web portal [1] and the eLecture-Portal of the University in Freiburg were developed (Her11b).

In order to go more into detail about facts and figures of tele-teaching web portals, the sample tele-teaching portal this work is based on will be introduced in the next section.

2.1.3   The Sample Tele-Teaching Web Portal tele-TASK

The sample tele-teaching portal used for the implementation of the functions developed in this work is the tele-TASK portal (www.tele-task.de) of the Hasso Plattner Institute (HPI). The Tele-teaching Anywhere Solution Kit (SM02), short tele-TASK, is an e-learning project at the chair Internet-Technologies and -Systems at the HPI. The project was started in 2002 at the University of Trier. tele-TASK was started with the development of a hardware system for lecture recording. Later on an all-in-one solution including hard- and software for lecture recording was developed. It is a plug-and-play solution. Two video streams (a video of the lecturer and a screen capture of his laptop or a smart-board) and one audio stream can be recorded at once with the hardware kit.

Most of the lectures recorded at HPI are available via the web portal tele-TASK, part of which was implemented during this work. More than 5000 lectures and 15000 podcasts of the tele-TASK archive can be accessed via the tele-TASK web portal (whose user interface is displayed in figure 2.3) or on a portable device. This large video archive and the web-platform are the basis for the research and development presented in this work.

The tele-TASK portal has been re-developed since 2009. The framework Django based on the programming language Python was chosen for the new implementation. A MySQL database is used in the backend of the portal. Because tele-TASK is a research project as well as the actual platform used by the students, the re-design required major thoughts about stability for the teaching context on the one hand and flexibility for research on the other hand. A loosely coupled plugin-architecture was developed, where each of the new features was implemented as a separate plugin (SMM10b). This allowed more researchers working on different parts of the portal while at the same time being able to guarantee a stable core version.

2.2   Engaging the Users

Tele-teaching was introduced as a solution that allows students to learn in a way that best suits their interests and needs, for example with respect to the speed of consumption. They can study independently from place and time. A large number of

---

[1]http://www.tele-TASK.de

14

Figure 2.3: Interface of the sample tele-teaching web portal.

students are in fact substituting the face-to-face lectures completely with e-lectures (RK11). Engaging the users into the learning process has been proven to be beneficial for students (Kir04, Sie05), though. Since especially tele-teaching is lacking the social interaction, because students mostly study individually at home, the user engagement is even more important in that context. Because user engagement if often low in institutional tele-teaching scenarios, this work will deal specifically with the topic of activating the users and making them participate. This task requires knowledge from different fields of study, which is why research from diverse disciplines will be presented and its relevance for tele-teaching will be discussed in this section.

Opportunities for user engagement improved tremendously with the invention and implementation of the Web 2.0 principles. Therefore, this section will start by diving into details about the utilization of Web 2.0 functions in tele-teaching. In order to catch the attention of a majority of the users, their specific learning styles need to be addressed. Which tools cater for which learning styles will therefore be presented in the following paragraph. This section ends by explaining which tools can be used to support which learning styles.

2.2.1 Web 2.0 Features in Tele-Teaching

Instead of focusing on content consumption in e-Learning, the Web 2.0 principles have brought up the idea of collaborative content creation and content sharing (Rei07, DHK+11). This opens up new potential for constructive, self-organized and collaborative learning, which benefits the learner (ML07). This new age of collaboration has also greatly influenced e-learning research and tool development (Mic06, SS08, DHK+11). This section will first deal with historical development of Web 2.0 in e-learning, then continues by elaborating the utility of Web 2.0 in e-learning even further and concludes with challenges this technological and societal development brings with it. Major parts of this chapter have been previously published in (GSM11, GM12, GYM+13a).

The History of Web 2.0 in Tele-Teaching Scenarios

The idea of Web 2.0 was introduced by Tim O'Reilly (Rei07) in 2007. One of the main ideas behind O'Reilly concept consists in users joining together to communities. Those users aim at the collaborative creation and sharing of media and web content. The joined force of the crowd is thereby able to generate larger amounts of data and feed it back to the crowd than it would be possible by individuals or administrative personnel.

Amongst the Web 2.0 functions that were researched and found helpful for the users are blogging, collaborative wiki creation, social tagging and annotation, recommending, content sharing and linking as well as evaluating (by rating or commenting). Statistical observations also showed that having fun in a community made an impact on people and resulted in the community growing tremendously (one example being Wikipedia). This is a potential, that can be leveraged for tele-teaching as well.

At the beginning of this century it was already proven that community function-alities are not only useful for private networking, but also in the learning context (PP99, Mic06, SS08). Research about joining tele-teaching with Web 2.0 function has started later, though. At the workshop *eLectures 2009* at the e-learning expert confer-ence of the German society of computer science (DeLFI) 2009 (TLH09), an approach of integrating tele-teaching applications into facebook (FENV09b) and other social e-learning scenarios were shown. The utilization of a rating function for e-lectures was elaborated in (MSM10a, MSM10b) in 2010. Utilizing Wikis with e-lectures was pre-sented in (Her11a) in 2011. The use of a tagging function together with e-lectures was described in detail in (MSM11a).

Utility of Web 2.0 in Tele-Teaching

Two perspectives on the utility of social web functions in tele-teaching can be taken. The first point of view is the one of a user benefiting from the social web func-tions in a tele-teaching environment. The second point of view is from the provider's side. Why should a portal developer be interested in offering Web 2.0 tools?

The learners are benefiting when their learning process is facilitated by the social web functions. The learning theory connectivism (Sie05), that is adapted to the digital age, supports this hypothesis that social interaction is beneficial for learners. And not only the social interaction in itself is a benefit. Also the outcome of the social interaction, the sharing of learning content, thoughts and discussions will improve the individual's learning. At the same time he might at some stage give knowledge back to the community and thus be helping fellow learners to advance further. A very good example of this procedure are programming forums, like Stack Overflow[1]. Whereas at the beginning users just consume the postings, they might later on post questions themselves and when having advanced in their learning might be answering requests of others and participate in the discussion.

Engaging the users through Web 2.0 functions will create a lot of textual data and metadata. This can help to improve the search, recommendation and filtering functions within the portals. When those core functions are more advanced and user friendly, the provider will benefit by being attractive to more and more users on the one hand and saving time and money on manual metadata production on the other hand.

When the single user becomes more active, the benefits for the community can be deducted from the connectivism theory as well. Knowledge sharing and connection building are of great advantage for the learning group as well. Furthermore, a lot more metadata is created, which can help to improve search, recommendation and filtering functionalities within the portal. A more user friendly interface will be advantageous for the community and also the providers, as more users can be attracted. The metadata

---

[1]http://stackoverflow.com/

production is further discussed in section 2.3. Other challenges will be reviewed in the next paragraph.

Challenges of Social Web in Tele-Teaching

Specifically local tele-teaching communities at universities or institutes quite often suffer from numerous problems. First, the number of the users is not as large as in the huge private and leisure oriented Web 2.0 platforms. With even a lot smaller number of students actually being active and collaborating, the knowledge sharing and connection only takes place amongst a small number of people (MT10). Without having the benefits of potentially hundreds and thousands of users replying to your issues or seeing your content, the incentives for participation decrease even more. So the participation in those small tele-teaching communities is generally low. A study about the Web 2.0 video service YouTube (CKR$^+$07) as well as experience with the example portal have made this problem evident.

The unity of those two issues leads to the main challenges of Web 2.0 implementation in tele-teaching: engaging more users and reaching a critical mass of user-generated metadata. In order to apply algorithms and foster user-generated metadata to provide additional functionality a minimal metadata base is required. Two classes of solutions can be taken into account for these issues. First of all the portal providers can try to engage users more into the community and animate them for more metadata creation. Second, automatic processes can be used to enhance and extend the user-generated metadata already existing.

Also the research paper of the e-learning group of the German society of computer science identified similar challenges for research. They found that it is necessary to research, how collaborative learning processes can be encouraged and supported. Furthermore it is required to know how Web 2.0 functions need to be implemented in order to support learning. And of course it is mandatory to know which tools can best be used in which learning situations, for which learning goals and contents and by which learners and teachers (DHK$^+$11).

The next section will introduce some thoughts about these issues in the newly emerged research area of Massive Open Online Courses. Afterwards, the topic of catering for different learning styles will be elaborated, before addressing participation and design guidelines.

2.2.2 Massive Open Online Courses

Massive Open Online Courses (MOOCs) are courses offered online that are open and target a very large audience. They aim at enabling a group of thousands of learners to learn together in a common space by offering tools and to some extend also content. The social interaction amongst the participants is regarded as key success factor for the learning progress of the individual learner in MOOCs. Therefore it is not surprising that the popularity and success of the MOOC model rose gradually with the dissemination of social networks and social media.

MOOCs are divided in two categories depending on their concept of openness (Rod13). Whereas all are open in terms of unrestricted access, they differ in their approach of openness of the learning process and the content. The categorization by Siemens (Sie12) divides the MOOCs into the xMOOC format that is loosely based on behaviourist pedagogy and traditional lectures and the cMOOC format that is constructed according to the connectivist pedagogical approach (Sie05). The xMOOCs usually use more or less closed predefined learning schedules and learning materials derived from their university's standard curriculum. On the contrary cMOOCs are more open in terms of schedule by allowing their learners to co-construct knowledge and learning processes by interaction with each other. They often use open educational resources to trigger and consolidate the group work. It was argued by Tony Bates (Bat12) that the xMOOC can very well be used to learn facts or procedures by using repetition, but that the higher level creative and critical skills can only be gained with the help of learning practices in the cMOOCs. The popular open xMOOC model was pioneered by professors at Stanford University (Ren13), but got his name from a platform operated jointly by Harvard University and the Massachusetts Institute of Technology (MIT), called edX[1]. The cMOOC model started off in Canada in 2008 driven by the two educational researchers George Siemens and Stephen Downes (GMTW13). The idea of educating a massive audience using communication technology and mass media is much older, though as is the notion of open access to education. Already the German *Funk-Volkshochschule*, founded in 1924, was based on this idea (Baa94). A more popular example of massive open education are German *Funkkollegs* (Gre98) which started in 1966 and distributed educational content via public radio stations. From 1967 on, *Telekollegs* that educated people via TV, books and face-to-face training were offered. In contrast to the definition of nowadays MOOCs, those did not take place online. The Telekollegs furthermore did not fulfill the criterion of being entirely open, because an entry fee, costs for the material as well as entrance requirements apply. A very popular example of open education is the Open University (OU) in the United Kingdom that was opened in 1970 (Kee96, PD13). It is open in terms of the entry requirements, but not open in terms of tuition fees.

In the xMOOC model, lecture recordings are the most important type of learning material used by the students to acquire knowledge. openHPI[2], the MOOC platform offered by the Hasso Plattner Institute, also follows the xMOOC model. Lecture recordings are, next to reading material and quizzes, the fundamental learning material that a majority of the students uses while taking the courses (GMM+13a), (GMM+13b),

---

[1] http://www.edx.org
[2] http://www.openhpi.de

19

(GMTW13). This is a parallel to the tele-teaching environments primarily addressed in this work. Therefore, the tools and methods identified can be used in either of these environments - tele-teaching or MOOCs. Furthermore, the identification of learning tools for certain learner types can be used as a quite general model independent from the learning platform or learning situation. Therefore the next section will introduce our scheme of matching learning types to learning tools and materials.

2.2.3 Catering for Different Learning Styles - Background in Learning Theory

Looking at e-learning and tele-teaching from the didactical and learner's perspective can be very enlightening for work in computer science, because how people learn, which types of learners there are and which learning settings those types of learners use, gives us many hints on the types of tools and technology required for these learners. When offering a very specific scenario in a framed kind of environment, like in a tele-teaching environment, will probably attract other kinds of learners than when offering a book or a lab environment. Thinking further, when we can expect a certain kind of audience with preferences in a certain learning style, we are also able to adapt the tools and technology offered according to their needs.

The analysis of the matching between learning styles and tools plus material for learning started off by collecting which tools were available in the MOOC system we were using and continued by thinking further about future tools to use. Tools and formats for presenting and learning the course material are lecture recordings, self-tests, homework and additional reading material. Those are complimented by tools for discussion. Those are typically blogs, social networks (like Twitter, Facebook), forums as well as learning groups (Rod12).

Learning Styles According to Kolb's Model of Experiential Learning

With those tools and formats in mind we looked at the experiential learning model of Kolb (Kol84), (KBM01) in order to determine which tools support which learning styles and thus to have a basis to decide on further requirements. Experiential learning specifies a didactical model that does not only include abstract theorization as major learning task, but a whole cycle of concrete experience, reflective observation, abstract conceptualization and active experimentation (Kol84). Those four phases are organized into two dimension: perceiving (from abstract to concrete) and processing (from reflective to active). Most learners can be categorized as preferring one of the four combinations of these two dimensions and thus belong to one of the following learning styles:

- Diverging Style: Learners using the diverging style combine concrete experience with reflective observation. They can best learn from examples and analyse these from different points of view.

- Assimilating Style: Assimilators combine the abstract conceptualization with reflective observation. Their preferred way of learning is from theoretical models.

- Converging Style: Learners with the converging style join the abstract conceptualization with active experimentation. This means they learn by carrying out ideas and concentrating on tangible problems.

- Accomodating Style: Accomodators utilize the concrete experience together with active experimentation. They favor learning by experimenting and adapt models to the experiences made.

Which Learning Styles Do MOOCs Currently Support?

Knowing the four different learning styles and the tools and methods currently available in our MOOC, we assigned those tools and methods to the four styles in the experiential learning cycle (see figure 2.4).

From this overview one can see, that xMOOCs predominantly help people with the assimilating style, because their main focus is on lecture videos, quizzes and reading material. The tools provided for the other learning styles, forums, learning groups and practical tasks are an add-on for the participants, but the majority of the learning process is focused on content distribution and individual repetition.

How MOOCs and Tele-Teaching Platforms Can Cater to All Learning Styles

Moving onwards and looking into how those traditional MOOCs can actually cater for more learning styles, we came to further tools that may support the learning process of the other styles. Those are based on literature on the one hand and feedback from the participants through surveys and feedback forms on the other hand. Participants in openHPI for example wished for more usage of animations, visualizations and simulations to support them in understanding complex topics. They also demanded to discover learning and information material beyond the platform. Therefore they suggested to use more extensive link collections allowing them to explore the information space further. Additionally the need for instant communication was expressed. Offering private and group chat functions is one offer the platform owners can provide in order to cater for this need. Finally a large number of participants demanded more practically relevant examples and exercises (GMTW13).

The reflective observation already has the majority of tools and methods on its side. Nevertheless the evaluation results of our survey as well as feedback from the

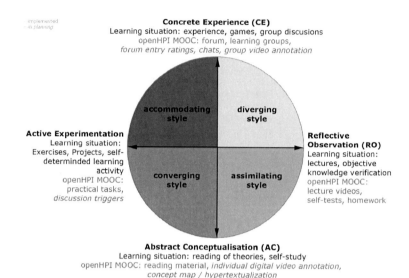

Concrete Experience (CE)
Learning situation: experience, games, group discusions
openHPI MOOC: forum, learning groups,
forum entry ratings, chats, group video annotation

implemented
- in planning

Active Experimentation
Learning situation:
Exercises, Projects, self-determinded learning activity
openHPI MOOC:
practical tasks,
discussion triggers

accommodating style

diverging style

converging style

assimilating style

Reflective Observation (RO)
Learning situation:
lectures, objective knowledge verification
openHPI MOOC:
lecture videos,
self-tests, homework

Abstract Conceptualisation (AC)
Learning situation: reading of theories, self-study
openHPI MOOC: reading material, *individual digital video annotation,*
concept map / hypertextualization

Figure 2.4: Mapping of learning tools to the four learning styles in Kolb's model (according to (Kol84) and (Sta05) pp. 67/70) of learning styles (GMM[+]13b), (GMTW13).

participants showed again, that consistent and properly prepared learning materials are very important for those learners. Glossaries can thus provide such structure and a quick reference for the participants. Using proper methods for self-reflection, like self-tests and a visual overview of the percentage of learning material worked through and points received can support the learners here.

The abstract conceptualization is only sustained by reading material in the MOOC we addressed. Here again it is important to have a cognitive orientation in the domain knowledge. Feedback from the students (GMM[+]13b), (GMTW13) as well as research in related areas (BÖ5), (AR03), (BCR11), (DD05c), (Hie05) revealed, that knowing the greater picture and inter-relations between topics is very important for students. Introducing concept maps is one way to cater for this need. A more heavy use of hypertextualization by cross-linking individual learning content pages and ideally even cross-referencing between videos is a second way to support students aiming to learn by finding their own learning paths. Abstract conceptualization may also be supported through note taking (HS07), (LYC[+]07).

Active experimentation can be supported by offering more hands-on experience for the students. Different types of scenarios can be thought of as addressed in

(GMM⁺13b), (GMTW13), (CW13), (WM12). In the example of one of the openHPI MOOC courses a tool called Wireshark was introduced in order to have the students find out how a certain Internet protocol works on their computer. The tool was introduced in a tutor video and students had to enter the results of their experiment in a matching quizz. The hands-on-experiences were heavily questioned in the forum (GMM⁺13b), (GMTW13).

The concrete experience dimension can be further supported by utilizing visualizations, simulations and experiments. Problem-solving and decision-making are key aspects that should be included in these tools. The research community is currently investigating how to scale those laboratories to a massive audience (WKR⁺11), (NP13), (GCV⁺).

As previously argued, tele-teaching environments are similar to MOOCs to some extend, as they are also based on lecture recordings, like the xMOOCs. Therefore some findings from the MOOC scenario how to cater for more learning styles can be transferred to the tele-teaching scenario. The active experimentation is a setting that cannot be transferred to tele-teaching. But concrete experience and abstract conceptualization can be transferred to tele-teaching and thus also supporting the accommodating and converging learning styles to some extent through the utilization of further tools. The main set of tools focused on in this work are video annotations, that support the abstract conceptualization, group video annotations, that support the concrete experience and concept maps including hypertextualization, that support abstract conceptualization and reflective observation.

Figure 2.5: Learning hierarchies according to Anderson and Bloom (For10)

Referring to the taxonomy of Bloom (see figure 2.5), students who use tools like the annotation and the concept maps will be lead to higher order thinking skills, by analysing what they learned and reflecting on how to go on on their learning path and synthesising what they learned in an overview of their own manuscripts.

What is missing in Kolb's model of experiential learning is the explicit characterization of the social dimension of learning (Whe12). The social dimension takes into account that learning takes place together with other learners in different kinds of contexts and social situations (BLS99). Researchers like Wenger even argue that in order to understand knowledge and created meaning, learners actually need to be an active member of a learning community (Wen98). The Internet and technology in distance education have thereby enabled students to collaborate despite the physical separation (OL06). Kolb's four learner styles can actually each be seen in a social dimension by expanding his model into a third dimension, which is the social one. The two sides of the axes would be individual learning and group learning, depending on the setting where the learning takes place. For example, when discussing about theories they just read, students in the abstract conceptualization mode will deepen their concepts with the help of those social interactions. Practical tasks and experiments may also take place for individuals or in groups. When students query each other with questions they created, they are on the highly social end of the third axis, whereas when they fill out multiple choice quizzes they are on the other.

Nevertheless the social dimension is not addressed explicitly in Kolb's model. We believe that by explicitly utilizing guidelines that cater for the social dimension and encourage participation, this gap can be overcome. The next section will therefore address the issue of participation in e-learning and go into detail about one solution to the problem - the culture of participation concept by Gerhard Fischer (Fis11).

2.2.4 Establishing a Culture of Participation as Means for Collaboration

In order to establish a culture of participation, current state of research concerning participation in e-learning will be explicated first. Afterwards, the culture of participation in our sample tele-teaching portal is analysed as one case of local university tele-teaching platforms and their degree of participation. Finally, an approach to improve active participation when using e-lectures is proposed. Most of the findings described in this chapter were previously published in (GM12).

The Didactics Behind Collaboration in E-Learning

Disadvantages of the traditional learning culture, like a fixed curriculum, mostly synchronous learning in groups and the dependency of students on the teachers' methods and choice of material have been overcome with the rise of e-learning. Open and flexible learning scenarios are now supported by e-learning technologies. Therefore, the new learning culture supports constructive and self-organized learning in fluid networks (Kir04). Traditional learning theories like constructivism (Fos96, DK07), cognitivism (Bru66) and behaviourism (Ski54) (a comparison of which can be found in (EN93)) cannot instantly explain these new learning scenarios because of a lack of consideration of technology supported learning (Sie05).

Connectivism (Sie05), a learning theory adapted to the digital age, describes learning as the creation of connections between mental constructs. Learning in a group can be very supportive for learners according to this theory, because a learning group can help forming these connections between knowledge. And Web 2.0 tools, like tagging, are ideal tools to be used for knowledge connection as well. The "cycle of knowledge" as described in the connectivist theory implies that learners on the one hand contribute knowledge to a learning community, but on the other hand gain knowledge from that community as well. Those benefits of the collaborative knowledge creation are the core idea of the Web 2.0 philosophy.

Although cooperation has been proven to be such an effective learning method, participation of students is often still very low (GM12). Part of the problem is the way the participative e-learning systems are designed. Therefore the next sections will deal with participation in e-learning and how it can be fostered.

Participation in E-Learning

Participation in online platforms and specifically in e-learning communities was researched intensely. Hostetter and Bush showed in 2008 that group learning positively influences the individual student's motivation and ambition to engage more strongly in academic activities. User satisfaction and social presence were measured in their study. The researchers found a strong correlation between both, which means that students feel more positive towards their learning when they have the sense of belonging to a group. However, the learning outcomes could not be correlated to this feeling of social presence. (HB08)

Kimmerle and Cress evaluated the information-exchange dilemma of an individual in a collaborative process in 2007. The task was to collaboratively work on a database. The individual only had more work and no immediate benefit from his participation. But only with the engagement of a lot of group members the group was able to perform at its best. A group-awareness tool was utilized to solve this dilemma for the individuals. This tool was utilized as an opportunity for self-presentation. When having received individual feedback by other participants, the individual group members were more willing to engage themselves (KC07).

Fischer defined the term culture of participation (Fis11) and suggested design guidelines supporting those cultures. The major goal is to stimulate participation. Three main design components are proposed. The first is meta-design, where collaborative design is enabled by the infrastructure. The second is social creativity, which means that by collaboration a group of participants are enabled to solve problems. The third is different levels of participation. Those levels shall allow diverse degrees of engagement by the participants, from consumer to meta-designer (see figure 2.6 for a detailed overview of the participation levels). Learning as an area where the culture of participation principle can be applied, is briefly discussed by Fischer. Learners should thereby be encouraged to work on explicit problems and engage in genuine activities. They furthermore should be inspired to learn by discussing and developing ideas and topics as shared understanding. Intrinsic motivation is the basis for participation. Motivation will be encouraged further when contributors feel support from the group and also see a common sense within the group (Fis11). The design guidelines proposed are one possible way to improve participation and will thus be investigated further in this work.

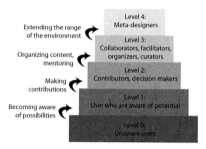

Figure 2.6: Levels of participation in a culture of participation (Fis11, GMTW13).

Utilizing the culture of participation framework by Fischer, Dick and Zietz analysed different motivation techniques within this culture. They identified peer pressure, social norm and social proof as most important motivational factors within sociotechnical systems. Again, awareness is the key to trigger these motivation mechanisms. By publicly displaying the activities of the group members, the awareness can be improved. Dick and Zietz conclude that it is a major task for designers of socio-technical systems to make users aware of their contributions and the contributions of their peers instead of trying to make them more active (DZ11).

Analysis of the Culture of Participation in Tele-Teaching Portals

In this section the culture of participation in a large sophisticated sample teleteaching web portal will be analysed. This sample tele-teaching web portal was briefly introduced in section 2.1.3. This section thus starts by briefly showing a statistical overview of the current usage of Web 2.0 tools in the sample tele-teaching portal. Afterwards, the current state of the application of the culture of participation principles is elaborated. Finally, a solution to foster active engagement is presented.

Studying an Existing Tele-Teaching Web Portal Web 2.0 functionalities in the example tele-teaching web portal have been researched for quite some time.

User-generated playlists (SMHM10), simple user-generated time-based annotations (GSM11), tagging (MSM11a), rating (MSM10b, MSM10a) and the creation of links to content items were implemented and partly researched (GSM11). A brief overview of a statistics of usage data of the community functions in the portal is given in table 2.1.

Community Functionality	Users Participating	Number of Items Created	Items by Top 5 Users
Links	0.6%	20	75%
Playlists	1%	430	44%
Annotations	0.4%	1288	97,8%
Tags	1.4%	650	94,3%

Table 2.1: User activity with community features in the portal (GM12).

The percentage of users actually participating in the creation of user-generated data in addition to the e-lecture metadata is very low. The number of users intensely utilizing these functions is even lower. Considering Fischer's ecology of participation (see figure 2.6 and (Fis11) for details), this means that only a small number of users actually is willing to ascent upwards from level 0 to a more advanced participation level.

Status Quo of The Culture of Participation   While working on our own tele-teaching portal, a lot of insights on existing functionalities and methodologies could be gathered. Based on those the relevance of these functions and methods for the culture of participation shall be analysed in this section. Using examples from the sample tele-teaching web portal, different possibilities for students to engage in the different levels of participation (as explained in the culture of participation theory (Fis11)) in a tele-teaching environment will be explained. Afterwards, an analysis of the portal according to the design guidelines for a culture of participation by Fischer (Fis11) as well as Dick and Zietz (DZ11) will be carried out.

Analysing the different levels of possible participation in tele-teaching (summarized in table 2.2), it could be seen that from the teacher or provider side a lot more opportunities need to be created. The collaboration and participation possibilities for students with the e-lectures created by the teaching staff is still restricted to a basic level. Either the teaching material has to be provided by the teachers or very complex learning scenarios have to be introduced if students should be engaged in content creation.

The implementation of the design guidelines for a culture of participation (Fis11, DZ11) is analysed next. Again the sample tele-teaching portal, which incorporates the most well-known features and methods for this kind of software, is used for the analysis. An overview of the application of the design guidelines is given in table 2.3.

Level of Involvement	Examples from a Tele-Teaching Environment
level 0: unaware consumers	Users only watching the e-lectures without being aware that there is more to it are unaware consumers. They don't know that they can create additional metadata or in some scenarios even be involved in the development of e-lectures.
Level 1: consumers aware of possibilities	Moving up to level 1 in the ecology of participation involves knowing that it is possible to influence for example the impact of a lecture by rating it, adding links to it or annotating it with meaningful tags or sentences. Aware consumers are maybe utilizing some of the user-generated content via the search function, but do not actively participate.
Level 2: contributors, decision makers	When moving from only knowing about the possibilities to actually becoming active, the users move to the next level of being a contributor. This behaviour is supported by functions like for example rating, tagging and the creation of links.
Level 3: collaborators, facilitators, organizers, curators	Mentoring other learnings and organizing content themselves moves users from the state of a contributor upward to a facilitator and organizer. However, a tele-teaching environment is usually not designated to enable mentoring of other learners. Being content organizer is possible though. A student may re-organize content privately or even make it accessible to everyone through playlists.
Level 4: meta-designers	In closed tele-teaching environments the option of meta-design is not intended either. Only the staff is able to add new functionality to a portal. Open spaces or upload fields allowing students to add own content is often not permitted due to security issues. In open source systems, like Moodle, students are even able to develop their own add-ons, but still the deployment depends on administrators and developers. Using purposeful didactical scenarios can enable students to be meta-designers and to contribute own content by including video productions to the learning outcomes. This production can either be focused on the content itself (see (CA13) as an example) or also on the presentation skills of the students (see (REM11) as one example).

Table 2.2: Different levels of participation in tele-teaching (GM12).

The tables 2.2 and 2.3 provide an overview of the current status quo of a culture of participation in tele-teaching systems. In order to in fact employ a proper culture of participation quite a number of steps are missing. First of all opportunities to move upwards from level 2 to the levels of coordination, collaboration and meta-design in the ecologies of participation are lacking. Second, possibilities for students to engage in problem-solving and online discussion are not yet well developed apart from a few examples. Third, mechanisms for group awareness and awards yet have to be established. Fourth, since underdesign is already present, it is likely that emergent behaviour will appear. If the learning design was developed in such a way that broadening the scope

Design Guideline	Realization in a Sample Tele-Teaching Platform
support different engagement levels	The previous table 2.2 discussed this design guideline in detail.
support human-problem interaction	Because tele-teaching is mostly focused on distributing learning materials and does not actively encourage involvement, human-problem-interaction is also not assisted strongly. Thinking about problems might be encouraged through using the annotation function in a proper learning scenario. An example of the implementation in a blended-learning-scenario, where students in teacher training used video annotations to discuss their own teaching, was shown in (REM11).
underdesign for emergent behaviour	As already explained in the previous table about participation levels, tele-teaching environments in formal learning settings at universities are quite closed. The possibilities for collaborative work, information exchange and discussions between participations are limited. This in itself is already underdesign that may encourage the learners to think about their own learning tools as well as processes and expand their learning activities beyond the platform or away from the given tools.
reward and recognize contributions, group-awareness	The learning scenario is one opportunity to acknowledge and honour participation. This might be achieved by contributions being graded, by peer review or involving the group in the individual participants' evaluation. The system does not support this kind of awareness mechanism so far.
feeling that behaviour is being judged	Recognising participation, which was mentioned in the previous row, is the basis for the feeling that participation in the group is evaluated by fellow group members. Because collaboration itself is sparse at the moment and awareness mechanisms to notice the involvement of others are not yet implemented, also the feeling of being judged cannot come up.
co-evolution of artefacts and the community	At the moment the system designers are separated from the students. Therefore a cross-pollination between the community and resources for system development is not supported. Users may only send requests and questions in order to negotiate the future system development.

Table 2.3: Realization of the design guidelines for a culture of participation (GM12).

of the learners beyond the platform is not desired, an open space should be prepared that allows learners to bring in their own tools and strategies. The co-evolution of community and system artefacts is also missing. This is difficult to realize in a university setting, though. The university needs to ensure availability and reliability of the system if it is a crucial or well utilized part of the curriculum. Quality assurance and development life cycle management will become issues when students become system designers.

The next section will introduce some ideas how to utilize the identified weaknesses in order to foster a culture of participation.

An Approach to Improve Active Engagement by Establishing a Culture of Participation

In order to enable a culture of participation in education and learning Fischer states that a framework for learners that allows discussing in groups, creating a common understanding and learning from real activities and problems needs to be established (Fis11). This section will briefly lead to one solution space that fosters participation according to the criteria defined in the previous section. First, functions that fulfil the criteria to be implementable in a group mode and may therefore be a starting point for a culture of participation are listed.

Collaborative functions in tele-teaching environments can be separated in time-independent and time-bound activities. Tagging of whole videos, creating playlists, forums as well as chat functions are time-independent activities. Time-bound activities are annotation functions utilizing a timeline approach. Setting time markers to bookmark specific positions within a video and also textual or multimedia video annotations belong to the time-bound activities.

A proven beneficial function for students is the digital annotation (Pri04, HHF09, Zup06, SYHZ10, YCS04, REM11). Collaborative notetaking and lecture video annotations help to overcome the disadvantages of the instructor-centric nature of learning scenarios with lecture videos by fostering active learning (Pri04). Textual annotations furthermore support the user in browsing the video content. Considering that annotations are a key factor in supporting hypertexts and hyper-documents (Mar98, Lan06), annotations are also a key function in supporting networked learning, like it is proclaimed in the connectivist theory. Next to free-text annotations also links and other media formats like images can be used as annotation (HHF09).

Not only the outcome of the annotation process, the additional metadata and content, are constructive for the user. Also the annotation process itself is helpful for the learning process. Annotating means that the students perform actions of interpretation, weighting and reflection of the content (HHF09). Therefore the digital annotation leads to a deepened understanding of the topic (Zup06). Those time-based annotations may furthermore be used as anchors for content-related discussion as opposed to forums. They may thus encourage further participation (Zup06).

In summary the digital annotation is the most profitable function in connection with e-lectures, because deep discussion, reflection and interpretation processes are triggered. Therefore the digital annotation function is suggested as starting point to transpose the culture of participation. The implementation chapter in section 3.2.4 will thus explain in detail how a culture of participation can be fostered within the digital annotation function.

2.2.5 Collaborative Digital Video Annotation

The research about standard video annotation functions has been in progress for more than ten years now (LG00, YCS04, ZHF⁺05, O'N05, Zup06, SW08, YPDD12, MKB10, Her11a, REM11, Sei13).

With the idea of the Web 2.0, collaborative and participative learning technologies were moved more in the center of research interests again. Also tele-teaching scenarios were broadened to enable collaboration amongst and participation of the students. The social virtPresenter project for example integrates the lecture recordings into a social network (FENV09b, FENV09a, Fox11). A plugin for facebook was written, which allowed students to see which other people are watching the video at which timestamp in the same moment they are watching the video. Furthermore interaction possibilities were offered. Those were discussion forums, time-based comments and a wiki-like tool called whiteboard. Those functions were evaluated by questionnaires (Spa09). Generally the social virtPresenter was evaluated quite positively. Functions used by the students were playing the videos, navigating with the videos and full screen mode. Seeing where other students are currently watching the video was partly adopted. Mertens et al. (MKB10) proved that the social navigation function influences the behaviour of future users and is regarded positively by the students. The features belonging to the collaborative part, like the discussion forum, chat and inviting friends, were nearly not used at all. Some students did not like the lack of privacy and embedding the tool in a social network at all.

Also Wilk et al. (WKE13) implemented collaborative video annotation tools within a social network. They incorporated an annotation environment within Facebook that allows annotating the whole video, scenes or objects within the video with links, videos, images or textual annotations. Those annotations were partly pre-build by the developers and partly done by the students. Collaborative work with the video was also enabled. The evaluation showed that group interactions with videos are essential for successful learning with social videos. The users most liked the possibility to navigate between information nodes. Nevertheless they found that the positive learning effect of pre-build information within the video was decreasing the longer the duration of the video. They also argue that the knowledge construction is improved using their social video. But they used a within-groups-design which might not be reliable due to the small number of test persons used. Still, their idea of a social video interface that joins the presentation and authoring environment is promising and should be investigated further.

Privacy and security are the major disadvantages of using private social network accounts for learning related tasks. The reason being that in social networks the user is not the customer, but the product, because that is the way how social networks earn their money (Rus11). Data security and people's right to privacy is already a major discussion concerning learning platforms like Moodle (SOĐ08, KD11) that are used within universities only. Also the new research field of learning analytics opens new discussions on privacy. Letting students act in a mostly foreign platform most probably even with their real name will exceed most universities privacy regulations and is thus not a suitable procedure for teaching and learning. Therefore it is more interesting if the positive social effects that can be achieved in well-known social networks such as Facebook can also be transferred to university internal scenarios that are aligned with privacy and security regulations. This work aims at investigating this aspect.

Steimle et. al (SBM09) introduced a paper-based collaborative tool for the annotation of lecture slides. They argue that a majority of students prefers writing on paper rather than using electronic equipment for annotating lecture videos. Arguments such as lower cognitive load and an intuitive use of paper together with evidence from a field study were taken as motivation to combine an analogue script writing scenario with the benefits of digital documents. The study is from 2009 and the use of laptops and tablet devices has heavily increased and will potentially increase more (sta13, Lum12). Furthermore the ease with which students use these devices (BAMD13, FSG13) has increased as well. Therefore the study would probably perform quite differently if repeated again nowadays. That is why this work aims at investigating digital video annotation versus analogue manuscript writing again. The evaluation of the collaborative aspect, also discussed in (SBM09), shows evidence for higher learning effects when the social functions are used. This effect wears off more and more the longer the video is.

LeeTiernan and Grudin (LG00) found that engagement and the usage of the annotation environment can be improved in a collaborative mode. The participants created a lot more annotations in a distance learning mode than in a live mode, which is an interesting finding since lecture recordings are often used in an distant asynchronous mode (Zup06). This work therefore aims at investigating whether the more intense writing of annotations may also be linked to an improved learning of the lecture's content.

Zahn et al. (ZHF+05) investigated collaborative learning video application in schools. Their tool allowed school kids to hyperlink, add information to, collect and discuss the videos, either while being in the classroom or via distance learning. They showed evidence that groups working collaboratively with the video outperformed those students that did not. Higher order cognitive skills are related to this process as it moves the student from a consumer to an author. Those findings are very interesting since they can be linked to learning theory advertising for more active learning which will lead to better learning outcome. Therefore this work aims at researching whether this active role is also beneficial for university student's learning. Zupancic (Zup06) gives a detailed overview of the usage of lecture videos including an annotation system. An evaluation of the annotation system was not conducted, though. Therefore the proof of concept is missing. Seidel researched the usage of a CSCL script in order to structure the collaboration process with lecture video annotations (Sei13). The approach was partly successful in balancing the participation of individuals. In this approach the annotation environment was specifically prepared for a certain learning scenario. In this thesis the focus should be on a general tool to support remote lecture recording consumption as well as live lecture content aggregation support, though. Therefore the scripting approach does not apply since it requires more preparation effort for the individual scenario.

A very popular tool for creating digital video annotations are wikis. Sack and Waitelonis (SW08) utilized a wiki to extend their academic search engine Yovisto. They also enabled collaborative video annotation via tagging of lecture segments. Both, students and lecturers, could use those tools meant for further discussion and explanation about the lecture videos. Because their wiki content was not time-based, re-visiting specific points within the video when the note was taken was not possible. As opposed to this approach the tagging feature is time-based, but does only allow short text inputs, which may limit the user wanting to write a lecture manuscript rather than only providing video metadata. A wiki solution to provide lecture video annotations was also suggested by Hermann and Ottmann (Her11a). They linked a specific point in the video with a wiki entry and used those entries as starting point for discussions. This functionality was evaluated positively by users and experts. Nevertheless the workflow of entering the annotations in the video is quite hard and time consuming, which may make it difficult to apply the approach in a live lecture setting. A very interesting approach to save time while creating a lecture script was introduced by O'Neill (O'N05). A lecture skeleton that was automatically extracted from the slides was copied to a wiki. The students were then asked to enhance this script. Unfortunately again this script was not time-based and the evaluation of the approach is missing.

The approach chosen for the annotation environment in this thesis will be designed to overcome some of the disadvantages of previous approaches. It will be targeted for the use in formal learning contexts, based on lecture recordings, although it may be used in informal learning scenarios as well. The annotation tool will be implemented in a dedicated tele-teaching environment of a specific institutions in order to avoid security and privacy issues that would arise in company-based social networks.

In a university setting students are bound to learn on a lecture basis to some extend anyway. Therefore the focus of the annotation tool lies on the application with lecture recordings. The usage of those lecture recordings in a live presence mode or on demand remote will be researched. Because the previously build wiki approaches are either not time-based or have difficult workflows, the approach in this thesis will include direct annotation of individual lectures by saving discrete points within the lecture. This will allow the additional benefit of a summarizing lecture manuscript creation for the user.

Finally, the annotation environment build in this thesis will be based on an open annotation input field without pre-defined vocabulary from the Semantic Web. This is necessary to omit possibly troublesome workflows and too much effort for the users and enable immediate benefit for them. The advantages that the Semantic Web could give to user-generated data are manifold. They render the data easier to harness for

33

search, navigation and filtering. Therefore the user-generated Social Web data will be connected to the Semantic Web.

2.3 Collecting Metadata and Making It Accessible

The rise of the internet and especially the Web 2.0 era have led to huge amounts of resources and data available for learning. This results in some challenges for the learners, who have limited time available and somehow need to find the content they are looking for in the mass of data. Even in small tele-teaching environments the amount of data is huge due to recording technology becoming cheaper as well as easier and faster to use. Distributing these masses of e-lectures-content to a massive audience is already solved and has been proven to work efficiently in MOOC scenarios (see section 2.2.2 for more information on MOOCs). Large amounts of those e-lectures are only being stored in a video format and manpower is still required for post production and metadata creation. This is a very time-consuming process. But when no additional metadata, like title, date of recording, the name of the lecturer and a content description enrich the actual media file, the possibility to find the desired e-lecture in a large number of recordings is decreasing. It is therefore still necessary to work on the problem of search and filtering in tele-teaching archives. Several options how metadata can be created or collected exist. Those will be summarized in this section. Parts of this section have been previously published in (MSM11b, GM13).

2.3.1 Metadata Sources within the Tele-Teaching Application

Tele-teaching data has one main characteristic that differs from most other e-learning content: it is multimedia. Because it is multimedia content, search and filtering processes without any additional metadata are quite difficult. Providing administrative metadata is the easiest and most used option to enhance the metadata basis for search and filtering processes. Due to the large amount of e-lectures recorded nowadays, this manual effort is very time consuming and costly though and is not feasible anymore when the amount of e-lectures recorded grows rapidly.

Different solutions to this problem exist. First of all the users can be integrated in the metadata creation process by allowing them to rate, tag and annotate the videos. This approach was explained in the previous section 2.2. A second solution is the automatic metadata harvesting. which will be explained in this paragraph.

Different parts of a tele-teaching environment may be distributors for content-related keywords (see figure 2.7 for an overview of modules that can be providers of keywords). First of all the *core* module can provide keywords retrieved from title or description information inserted by administrative personnel. The *search* module is a second module having access to important keywords in a tele-teaching portal. Keywords that users are searching for and the frequency they have been searched for are known by the search module and can therefore be utilized for the retrieval of additional metadata, but not primarily to retrieve videos directly.

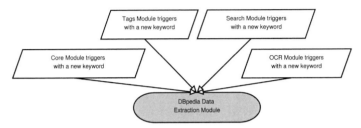

Figure 2.7: Different modules in the portal triggering the semantic context extraction process for their keywords (MSM11b, GM13).

Automatically harvested metadata, for example from the speech or from the image data of the video can be used as another solution to the lack of metadata problem. An automatically generated extracted textual outline from the images in the video is one example. This outline is generated by automatically segmenting the video into distinct content blocks, where the final frame of that block (mostly the final slide that has been built up after a series of animations) is used to apply optical character recognition on it to extract the title data (YGM12). With the help of this automatical segmentation, a preview of the slides can also be offered, which helps the indexing of the video for the users (YGBM13). OCR transcripts together with automatic speech recognition transcripts of the speech can be used to provide keywords to the videos (YGBM13).

In order to extract valuable content-related keywords from the video data itself, algorithms to harvest the most essential information with the help of OCR and ASR have to be applied. Afterwards, the information needs to be aggregated and actual keywords need to be extracted from the aggregated data. The same procedure is necessary for keywords that should be utilized from the title or description information.

All these keywords, collected by different modules in the tele-teaching portal, will be provided to a module that retrieves further information about them automatically. This is done with the help of Semantic Web methods. Basics of the Semantic Web and how semantic keyword information can be gathered will be described in the next paragraph.

2.3.2 External Metadata Sources - The Semantic Web and Tele-Teaching

The vision of the Semantic Web is to be able to join existing knowledge and do reasoning of that knowledge with the help of logic applied. This, so the vision, will lead to computers being able to give answers to questions for mankind that exceeds the human knowledge alone, answers to questions that were not previously answered. By combining common knowledge from diverse fields of expertise and thereby creating new knowledge this vision should be tackled. The goal is to enable machines to answer semantically comprehensive queries. Decades of research have followed this vision. Around this field of problems the idea of the Semantic Web was born (BLHL01, BKLI07).

The intersection of the Social Web with the Semantic Web has been researched previously (Gru07b). This connection between the social and the semantic world is especially useful to bridge the gap between unordered social data and structured data (Gru07a). It was identified that especially tagging data is valuable to bridge that gap. This paragraph will introduce the basic idea of the Semantic Web, of the linked data initiative. One linked data project - DBpedia - will be introduced as well. Next, an overview will be given of research combining the Social and Semantic Web with e-learning. This paragraph concludes by discussing the utility and challenges of Semantic Web in e-learning.

The Semantic Web

The World Wide Web Consortium (W3C) has published several open standards for the Semantic Web (BKLI07) . Amongst those are especially XML, RDF (Schema), OWL, SKOS and SPARQL. Those allow it to publish data in a meaningful manner in the form of taxonomies or ontologies and query these, for example RDF-ontologies with the help of SPARQL. Resource Description Framework (RDF)[1] is a formal language allowing to describe structured information. It is used to (semi-)structure, interchange and expose data on the Web. An RDF document is a directed graph that is built up of a number of knots and edges. In order to describe an RDF graph, each edge is written in the form of a triple (subject, predicate, object). Those triples can be written in XML syntax and describe relationships between semantic entities. Each of those knots and edges can be uniquely identified by the Uniform Resource Identifier (URI). The URI is the address under which the descriptions of the resource, that is identified by that URI, can be found. It must not necessarily link to a valid web address though, its main purpose is the unique identification of a resource. URIs, triples and RDF can thus be used to describe basic entities and their relations in the Semantic Web. The description of the entities itself is presented in the RDF format and contains

---

[1]http://www.w3.org/RDF/

36

information about the resource as well as links to related resources. URIs will deliver the format required by the user agent accessing it. When queried by a Semantic Web agent RDF data will be given back. When approached by a standard web browser, the same information will be returned in an HTML format.

RDF Schema[1] (RDFs) is a vocabulary description language and a semantic extension to RDF. RDFs provides basic classes that allow to start working with the triples by describing groups of entities that are related and relationships between these. Classes are types or categories. Other vocabulary description languages, like OWL or SKOS are built on RDFs. The W3C Web Ontology Language (OWL) is a language based on logic within the Semantic Web. It can express information about individual things, groups of things and relations between things. Knowledge represented in OWL can be reasoned with by software. Documents written in OWL are known as ontologies. OWL is as well represented in triples. It can be used to express more complex properties and classes, like a parent-child-relationship or that something is the same. The Simple Knowledge Organization System[2] (SKOS) is another application of RDF schema. It allows representing the basic content and structure of concept schemes such as taxonomies, folksonomies and other.

Linked Data

Linked Data summarizes the efforts of interconnecting data. It technically means that data is published on the web in machine-readable way and thus allows linking different data sources. More specifically it means data that is on the one hand published so that it can be referred to from other data sets, but also links to other data sets itself. It is based on two main technologies: RDF and URIs (BKLI07, BHBL09).

For the vision of the Semantic Web to be fulfilled, big data sets needed to be provided to researchers for experimenting and developing. The Linking Open Data Project[3] was founded by several research groups together (BHBL09) in 2007 and is supported by the W3C. They were later on joined by larger organizations and institutions. Their aim is to identify data sets on the web, transfer them to a machine readable format according to the Linked Data principles and publish them. Their goal is also to provide researchers an overview of available datasets and publish more resources and descriptions on the web for active use.

One part within the Linked Data initiative is DBpedia. Utilizing Linked Data methods, the goal of the DBpedia founders is to convert the content of the popular community-driven online-encyclopaedia Wikipedia into structured knowledge to make it accessible for machines (BKLI07). To transfer this data to a semantic form two different techniques are applied. In a first step the relationships between different

---

[1]http://www.w3.org/2001/sw/wiki/RDFS
[2]http://www.w3.org/2001/sw/wiki/SKOS
[3]http://www.w3.org/wiki/SweoIG/TaskForces/CommunityProjects/LinkingOpenData

entities gathered from the database are mapped onto RDF. In the second step further information is gathered directly from the text on the sites, the text inside info boxes and articles. Due to that initiative the huge amount of data that was put together in a community effort now becomes accessible to machines. Being structured now, this knowledge base can be accessed by other applications via interfaces provided. Output formats for the raw data are CSV, RDF and OData. Next to DBpedia there are numerous other knowledge bases available in the Linked Data Cloud, like Open Calais and Freebase (BLK+09). But, because DBpedia is a very large database with a very broad range of topics (BLK+09) and because there exists other services which are tailored for it, DBpedia is the knowledge base that will be used in this work.

Individual items can be identified with the help of the URI. But when looking at standard text, keywords within the text first need to be mapped to a URI before semantic context can be found. Therefore the next paragraph will briefly introduce this task of Named Entity Recognition, disambiguation and entity linking.

Linking Unstructured Text to the Linked Open Data Cloud

When the advantages and opportunities of the Linked Open Data Cloud should be used for applications in e-learning there are two ways to do so. Either the learning objects can be annotated with Linked Data, like it is done in (YPDD12) from the start. Or it is necessary to link unstructured text utilized in learning objects to the Linked Open Data Cloud to then be able to utilize the connected data for further processing.

The process of finding semantic entities in user-generated annotations starts with named entity recognition. Named entity recognition identifies possible entities that may belong to a keyword within a free text. When looking at language it is obvious that certain words may have different meanings. For example when a biologist writes about python most certainly the type of snake is meant. Whereas when a computer scientist writes about python, most certainly the programming language is meant. In order to find out which of the meanings is meant, the context of the word within a text is considered. Otherwise a context may be pre-set. In our case a disambiguation process that considers the context is utilized to identify the correct entity within the Semantic Web. Finally when the entity is identified it is linked to the keyword by entity linking.

For those three tasks a service called DBpedia Spotlight was proposed (MJGSB11) that determines which DBpedia entity may belong to which keyword in a free text. Because this service is specifically written for the previously selected knowledge base DBpedia and because it received good evaluation results (RT11) this service is utilized for the implementation in this work (see section 3.3.2).

The next step for applications using this Linked Data is to find relations to other entities. Details about related entity finding are explained in the next paragraph.

Finding Relations Using Linked Data

When being able to find related entities to the entities mapped via DBpedia Spotlight, those connections can be used for further processing, like for recommender systems, showing the context of the term or other use cases. This is the case, because in this way other key terms can be detected that somehow have a relationship to the start entity. Being in relation means that somehow people interested in one of the two might be interested in the other as well. A very popular example of this scenario is the web shop Amazon[1]. When they sell an audio player they recommend related items on the same site. Knowing that in order to listen to music with an audio player either headphones or speakers are required, an obvious path is recommending those two as other items to buy together with the audio player. To find related entities for the entities connected to key terms in the users's annotation, several approaches can be used.

Entities can be considered as related

- if they are directly related, by being object and subject in a triple (NMO[+])

- if they belong to the same category, which is assigned by the properties *dc-terms:subject* and *skos:broader* (NMO[+]) (which can be part of any of the next two conditions)

- if they are both subjects of triples with the same property and object (NMO[+]), like for example objects belonging to the same type relation *rdf:type*

- if they are both objects of triples with the same property and subject (NMO[+])

- potentially if they are used in the same context (SS13, AMHWA[+]05)

Once potential candidates for related entities have been discovered, the degree of their proximity needs to be determined by ranking the relations.

Ranking Relations Using Linked Data

The degree of the closeness needs to be determined, because there are potentially large numbers of related entities. Because humans are not easily able to handle hundreds or thousands of recommendations, and because the knowledge how closely related the other items are helps judging the results, the degree of proximity between two entities needs to be calculated.

There are two major ways to calculate the semantic relatedness of two terms (LRQ12):

- by using co-occurrence models based on statistical methods to compare words within a text.

---

[1] www.amazon.com

- by defining the distance between words in a graph using ontologies.

One of the most well-known models in information retrieval, belonging to the first solution space is the Vector Space Model (VSM) (SWY75), which also belongs to the co-occurrence models. It has been used in many algorithms exploring the relatedness of entities in the Semantic Web (NMO$^+$, GM07, Men13). The VSM was originally developed for the use of information retrieval and language processing in text documents. It represents a text as a vector of identifiers, like index terms (SWY75). The weighting of these index terms is done by using term frequency (TF) and inverse document frequency (IDF) (SM83).

Amongst the first class of methods is furthermore the Latent Semantic Analysis (LSA) that utilizes word co-occurrences to statistically determine the relatedness of texts. Explicit Semantic Analysis (ESA) uses the representation of texts as weighted vectors of wikipedia-based concepts that can be compared with metrics like cosine similarity (ZM98) to gather the distance between texts (GM07, LRQ12). Di Noia et al. suggest an algorithm using the Vector Space Model (VSM), which was adapted to work with RDF graphs (NMO$^+$). It considers individual properties as factors for relatedness. Also Mendes et. al. (Men13) and Garcia-Silva et. al (GSJMB11) propose a relation finding algorithm in DBpedia using the VSM, considering again the words used in a DBpedia resource.

Transferring the VSM and TF-IDF scheme to the RDF graphs, especially to DBpedia, each resource is modelled in a vector of either words (when the content is considered) or properties (when the structure is considered). The TF value can then be used to measure the relevance of a word or a property for the resource, that means assigning it a weight. The IDF can be used to determine how specific this word or property is in the set of all DBpedia resources (AT05, NMO$^+$, Men13). The similarity of two entities can then be computed by taking the cosine similarity between the vector angles (NMO$^+$, ZM98, GM07, Men13). Because this method was extensively researched and quite good results have been received (NMO$^+$, Men13), this method was chosen as the first algorithm implemented in section 3.3.2.

Amongst the second solution space is the metric proposed by Moore et al (MST11). They find the shortest path between two entities by assigning each path between two entities a weight dependent on the degrees of the subject and object. The degree of an entity is the number of its categories and the degree of a category the number of its entities. The shortest path then is the maximized log-likelihood of a path during a random walk on the graph. This algorithm was chosen for the implementation in section 3.3.2, because on the one hand it found rather unexpected and thus interesting paths and neighbours and on the other hand it has good results in computation time (MST11).

It is quite often the case that a lot of things are technically possible whereas proper ways of application have not been thought of which is why the utility of the semantic keyword information will be dealt with next.

2.3.3 Utility of Semantic Keyword Information

The metadata collection is no purpose in itself. In a tele-teaching context the metadata collection has the aim to provide better and faster search and filtering options as well as more knowledge about the content to the user. It may also help in showing connections between different teaching units. In the world wide web users generally use search engines, like Google or Bing, to find the desired content. Websites usually offer a lot more possibilities to retrieve content within the site.

Menus and lists are the first entry points to a website. Those are used for navigating through the content. The menu usually provides the opportunity to browse through the predefined categories the content is arranged in. The users can mostly not influence the navigation, because it is determined by administrative metadata. When the number of items in the list becomes too large, the trouble starts for the user. Having to scan long lists, users might stop their search after a few pages without having reached their goal. Sub-categories are one way to solve this issue as long as the amount of sub-categories does not get too large. With very large amounts of data navigating via lists and menus will become too difficult. Additionally content classification into predefined categories is very time-consuming and might thus hardly be achieved with masses of data. Therefore, we have looked into automatical categorization approaches for tele-teaching data (GSSM12).

User-generated metadata, like tags, can alternatively be used for navigation. Using tags can provide possibilities for two sorts of problems - navigation and search. On the one hand tags are often used when the user finds interesting content and wants to browse further for content related to one aspect of it. On the other hand, not knowing precise words to look for, the user can use a tag cloud as inspiration for interesting topics and then search for related content items.

Navigation is not the only area of application for metadata. Also the search function, which is another entry point into big archives which is of great importance, requires metadata. The sample tele-teaching web portal tele-TASK provides two different search options. A simple ajax search combines as much metadata as possible and only needs the keyword as input. The advanced search allows the user to specify and combine different search criteria.

Searching for a special keyword without having semantic metadata, the user will only find equal results to those he would get, when he used a link in the tag cloud giving him all matches for exactly this one keyword. Utilizing semantic information, more results can be returned. Synonyms, generalizations and more specific keywords can be found additionally. Allowing a search interface to be adaptive, meaning to change its focus when the user clicks on a different aspect of the initial key term, the user interface can support serendipitous browsing.

A further navigation possibility are suggestions. This is a phenomenon widely used in e-commerce. Big web shops, like Amazon[1], will show related items to the item one is looking at in that moment or earlier on. This recommendation is based on the preferences of the user as well as the similarity between the items. Details about recommender systems in tele-teaching environments and how those may incorporate semantic information are explained in (MSM11b).

Using semantic information, those last three navigation types, that are dependent on metadata, can be enhanced. Incorporating information about generalization, synonyms and child relations, the search function, the recommender system and tag clouds can be improved.

2.3.4   Connecting the Semantic Web with E-Learning

In the last years the connection of the Social and Semantic Web with e-learning gained some research attention. Different ideas around this area were tried out and researched. This section will summarize some related work in this area.

Lucke und Martens (LM10) gave an overview of semantic technologies in e-learning. They described mechanisms that were developed, starting from the utilization of metadata for an improved accessibility via the application of ontologies for automated course generation to the utilization of semantic data inside a learning object. In this work the latter way of utilizing semantic data inside a learning object shall be followed.

One approach tried was to engage users into the creation of the semantic context (BBGM09). Users were asked to manually add relations between tags they assigned. The incentive for the users to participate should be to ultimately have better metadata and thus more exact search results. However, the evaluation results showed that not a lot of users took part in this activity. This technique was thus not considered to be very successful.

A second research aimed at involving students and teachers in the development of a domain ontology for their subject (TJB[+]08). The tags added by students served as basis for the ontology. A relatedness algorithm was used to compute, if those student's tags fitted into the domain ontology. This way teachers should be supported in creating a domain ontology. This method was judged as being very promising.

Another approach limited the annotations to a certain set of pre-defined vocabulary. It is mostly used for ontology-based or linked-data-based annotations, like described in (YCS04, YPDD12). The aim of the limitation of the vocabulary was to only use known semantic entities and thus enable machine-readable annotations and semantic search.

---

[1]http://www.amazon.com

From the student's perspective the process of annotation with limited vocabulary can be difficult, since they sometimes cannot decide for a term or sentence and do not know how many annotations they can apply (YPDD12). In some cases this can mean that the students invest a lot of time in thinking about which annotation to choose, often even with pausing the video, without having an immediate benefit themselves. Since they're limited to pre-defined vocabulary they do not have a summary of a lecture of another direct outcome. The benefit only appears later, when the annotations can be used for specific search tasks. Therefore the question remains if students would be willing to go through that process as a regular task. This was not studied so far. In this work thus should be refrained from utilizing the users of the system to do the semantic annotation.

A semantic search interface for an academic video search engine was proposed in (WSHK10). Thereby the search query was forwarded to DBpedia in order to build up an exploratory search interface. In the interface, semantic connections of the search term are suggested to the user in order to enable free browsing and serendipitous search results.

The goal of this work is not to build on administrators, users or teachers to create additional semantic metadata as it was done in the first publications explained in this section. Like in the last approach the automatic extraction of semantic information should be triggered. But whereas Waitelonis et al. start from the side of the search interface, this work will start from the learning content and associated metadata. This path was chosen, because it allows to utilize all the different metadata available in a tele-teaching portal. This work aims at applying an algorithm that leverages keywords within the learning content archive that were inserted either by information retrieval, administrators or user participation.

When a lot of metadata is available, it needs to be made accessible. Some ways to do so, which have been researched excessively, are search interfaces and recommendation systems. Another approach are visualization techniques, like tag clouds or topic maps. Because topic maps are standardized to visualize Semantic Web data, their implementation will be tackled in this thesis.

2.3.5 Employing Topic Maps to Visualize Semantic Metadata

Topic maps were initially defined by the International Organization for Standardization in 2000 (the current standard is ISO/IEC 13250-2:2006) and adapted to the internet by the TopicMaps.Org consortium in 2001 (XML01). They are a standard for modelling semantic networks and are thus suited to represent ontologies (PH02, DD05c). The aim of topic maps is the representation and annotation of knowledge about information resources. They thus allow navigation at a high abstraction level (GS02). Topic maps are build up out of *topics* which are related by *associations* and point to information resources via *occurrences* (information resources may for example be photographs or an entry in a encyclopaedia) (GS02).

Utility Topic Maps

The goal of topic maps is to help the users quickly locating the desired information and exploring its structure easily. Thus this graph-based information visualization may help the user gaining an overview of a structure and then be able to pick a topic he is interested in (GS02). Map-based interfaces help the user to contextualize information and improve the exploitation of resources (AR03). This feature of contextualization of learning content was already demanded by quite a number of users in a MOOC scenario and supports the abstract conceptualization in Kolb's model of learning styles (see section 2.2.3). Furthermore topic maps help to find and share learning content (DD05c). Map-based interfaces additionally support the notion of hypermedia (AR03), meaning that via the map-based interface the user is able to quickly navigate among content elements.

In e-learning there are approaches to use topic maps in order to be able to re-use learning objects in different learning scenarios (DD05c, LM10). This is possible by embedding them in a hierarchical structure on the one hand and in a networked structure such as a topic map on the other hand. Lucke and Martens (LM10) describe this approach by integrating topic maps with learning objects. The networked learning paradigm, which is supported with the topic maps, fits well to the connectivist approach explained in section 2.2.4. It allows explorative learning and self-directed knowledge construction (Hie05). Dicheva et al. (DDW05) also argue that topic maps on the one hand enable learners who know what they are looking for to efficiently and quickly retrieve the desired information whereas on the other hand learners who do not know what they are looking for are supported in explorative search.

Map-based interfaces can be generated by a human or computed automatically (AR03) as can be the underlying data structure. Quite often a software package is used that allows manual modelling of a topic map on the one hand and viewing the topic map on the other (MWC04, DD05c, Hie05, Pin10). In e-learning, the teacher and sometimes even the pupils will then be involved in the topic map modelling. Since topic maps represent a form of knowledge management this modelling process may even be used in a didactically purposeful way as learning task (Pin10, Hie05). Higher level reflection and self-organization skills are required from the students, which supports them in gaining skills from the top of Bloom's hierarchy of skills.

Other forms of maps exist for learning as well. Those are concept maps and mind maps. Whereas topic maps and concept maps explain relationships between topics, mind maps do not. Topic maps are based on at least one central topic whereas concept maps do not and mind maps do not need to. Concept maps are build out of nonhierarchical net structures whereas mind maps use the form of a tree diagram and topic maps are hierarchically structured (Pin10).

A topic map does not necessary need to be visualized in the form of a network (GS02). The representation may use different kinds of metaphors, like graphs, trees, maps and even virtual worlds. Those visualization techniques can be selected depending on the context of use and the level of detail required. The networked structure is quite popular in e-learning applications, though (Hie05, Pin10).

Topic Map Implementations in E-Learning

Lucke and Martens (LM10) brought up the question how learning objects can be arranged hierarchically on the one hand while being available for non-linear knowledge acquisition on the other hand. They describe the extension of the XML based eLearning Language $< ML >$ [3] (Multidimensional LearningObjects and Modular Lectures Markup Language) with the possibility of describing topic maps. Topic maps are a possible way of describing the connections between learning objects in a networked and thus didactically flexible manner. The main benefit is that the content remains untouched and can be re-used in a different context.

Dicheva et al. (DD05c, DDW05, DDL[+]06) propose an interface that supports editing and browsing of topic maps for e-learning. They describe relationships they allow to be modelled in the topic map. Those are the *part-whole relationship*, the *superclass-subclass*, the *class-instance*, the *related-to* and the *similar-to* (DDW05, DD05b, DD05a). Those considerations are used for this thesis when selecting which relations of an entity in the Linked Data cloud are being followed to find neighbour entities (see section 3.3.2 for details about the implementation). Furthermore they also offer structural information as well as documents and links in their topic map view in an integrated manner. As this design principle has been proven to work well for information search and retrieval tasks, it will be taken on for this work.

Manual topic map creation is a very time consuming and knowledge requiring task. It is therefore not the right solution for every learning scenario. As the information search use cases are one of the most important use cases for topic maps in tele-teaching, an automatic topic map data generation will be approached to be able to offer the users the benefits of having a topic map without having to go through the trouble creating it.

The idea of automating the creating of topic maps has first been addressed by the developers of Ontopia, Steve Pepper and Lars Garshol (PSGM). Their proposal utilizes structured or semi-structure data. Therefore it is not suitable for the tele-teaching context as the video data dealt with is build up of unstructured data.

A semi-automatic process to generate topic maps is introduced by Yang and Lee (YL03). They use the text mining algorithms as well as document cluster maps and word cluster maps to develop a hierarchical representation of a document. Since this paper was published a lot of progress made within the Semantic Web, meaning that large data sources with interconnected knowledge are already available and ready to use. Those knowledge networks have powerful querying possibilities, which is why those are preferred over the method of creating a hierarchical structure yet again for every new document. Furthermore using the Semantic Web will also allow visualizing relations to keywords which are not mentioned in the text, but also have a relation to the document. The Semantic Web is thus a more flexible method.

When totally automatic algorithms shall be applied on unstructured data, the whole process from linking unstructured text to the Semantic Web via finding relations to ranking relations in the Semantic Web has to be run through.

2.4   Discussion and Approaches

The initial research question for this work was how Web 2.0 and Semantic Web technologies could be utilized to improve the interaction of students with e-lectures. While researching it became obvious that many different work areas are related to this topic. Computer science, didactics and social aspects, like collaboration and participation theory concepts, needed to be considered for this research.

Looking at the different learning styles some tools could be identified that may further help learners from different learning styles to better work with e-lectures. E-lectures mostly cater for the concrete experience and abstract conceptualization styles of learning. This section summarized different tools existing in current tele-teaching environments to support these two learning styles and also suggested new features that could additionally be offered to the learners. Those are collaborative digital video annotation and concept or topic maps. The collaborative annotation function may also fulfil the purpose of activating students when utilized in the right learning scenario. This is necessary, because research in didactics revealed the importance of engagement and active participation of the students in order to achieve good learning results. When using e-learning this is often done in remote setups, where the student learns at home on his own. This may quickly result in a lack of activeness and collaboration due to the missing social surrounding. A lack of engagement might also occur during lectures with many students, when the lecturer does not use methods to activate the individuals. The digital annotation may also cater for this scenario, when a live lecture annotation tool is utilized.

Several lecture video annotation tools are existing already. But it has not yet been studied, if those annotation tools are in fact used by the students and which kind of functionality and process is useful and needed to make this kind of function a success for the students. Also we identified the need to study if utilizing a textual annotation function really helps the students to learn more while watching a lecture. Furthermore existing approaches utilize a Wiki, where specific points in a lecture need to be added to create an annotation, or where an annotation is added in form of linked data, which are both quite time consuming for the user. This work focuses on very basic annotation functions. Those are attached to a lecture, because in a university scenario the students are anyway bound to learn on a lecture basis. The aim was to develop two kinds of annotations, free-text and marker annotations. The first enables the user to write longer comments whereas the second allows an even quicker bookmarking of a point in time within the video with pre-defined texts. Those two varieties of annotation will be evaluated and compared. As additional novelty the annotation function should not only be usable for lecture that have already been recorded, but also for lectures that are just being recorded. The live versus the on demand scenarios will also be compared.

In this chapter it was furthermore argued that metadata was needed, why it was needed and where it could be retrieved from. The learning theory section with the connectivism as well as the section about external metadata sources with theory about the Semantic Web showed evidence for the growing requirement of having relations and connections between resources. Furthermore the growing research area of connecting Social Web data with Semantic Web methods was introduced. The utility of semantic keyword information in tele-teaching environments was also expressed. In this work the emphasis should be laid on using the user-generated data as trigger to query Semantic Web data sets and thus automatically retrieve the context of user-generated keyword data. Because different modules in a tele-teaching portal, like the tagging module, the search and the recommendations module, can make use of semantic keyword information, the framework suggested in this work will query the relation information and transfer it in the sample portal application for further application. A number of different methods to find neighbours to keywords in a semantic knowledge base were introduced. Since finally the ranking amongst those will decide, which of those are most valuable and will thus be used for further processing, all of the neighbour finding possibilities will be used together. For ranking neighbours there exist two major approaches: the Vector Space Model and the determination of distances between words in a graph using ontologies. In order to see which of those methods is most beneficial for the users in the context of tele-teaching, both will be implemented and compared. All methods will be utilized in conjunction with the knowledge base DBpedia, because it is a large dataset which covers a broad range of topics and has a number of additional services developed for it.

One application this work focuses further on are semantic topic maps. Topic maps have advantages for the learning process of the user, but their manual generation is very time consuming. Therefore this work aims at researching if standard retrieval methods from the Semantic Web can be employed in order to automatically generate these topic maps using the previously explained user-generated keywords. The hypothesis is that it is possible to automatically generate topic maps that help the users and that this approach holds the additional advantage that users can relate to the topic map content more when they see that the data they contributed is the basis for the topic map.

2. CURRENT STATE OF RESEARCH

Chapter 3

Implementation of User-Centered Tele-Teaching Tools

This chapter will deal with the implementation of several social and semantic web functions in a sample tele-teaching portal. First of all, the implementation of basic social web functions as well as a quick evaluation of those is explained. Due to the not very successful usage of those functions, the main focus of this chapter lies on the development of lecture video annotation tools, incorporating aspects of a culture of participation as well as a semantic topic map.

When looking at the implementation of the web 2.0 functions in the tele-teaching context, some specifics of e-lectures have to be considered. The content of e-lectures is divided into several layers that are interlinked (see figure 3.1). Relative to the university setting, the top level is the lecture series, that usually has the duration of one semester. Within the series, several lectures take place. Lecture recordings form the primary content layer. Those are the containers holding the media items, whereas the series are an organizational level above the lectures.

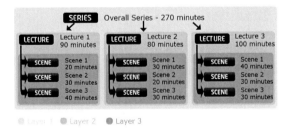

Figure 3.1: Content layers in tele-teaching portals

For reasons of convenience for the users utilizing mobile devices and in order to allow the consumption of small pieces of the lecture, the lecture recordings are split into scenes. Those scenes then can be distributed in form of podcasts on platforms such as iTunes U (GMMS10). Because of those content levels being different, there is a need to consider for each of the developed tools, which of the layers they were applied to best. With this in mind, the next section will deal with the implementation of basic web 2.0 functions in the tele-teaching portal.

3.1 Implementation of Basic Web 2.0 Functions

Amongst the most basic Web 2.0 functions, that can be found on nearly every web platform incorporating Web 2.0, are content rating, tagging and playlist functions. The implementation of those Web 2.0 tools in the tele-teaching context and some specific adjustments for the tele-teaching context will be explained in this chapter.

3.1.1 Calculating a Rating Functionality over Several Content Layers

Rating is the classification of content. This categorization is done to order or grade the content. In the context of tele-teaching, rating is the quantification of personally perceived quality of an item. Rating is the easiest to use Web 2.0 function. As users only need to click on typically one out of 5 stars to evaluate an item (see figure 3.2), this is a very quick and easy process that users might be more willing to use than more time-consuming Web 2.0 functions, like supplying own content. Content filtering and recommendation engines may then utilize this rating information by the users to provide the best rated results.

Figure 3.2: Two different views of the rating function in tele-TASK

When implementing this function in a tele-teaching context, the three different content layers have to be taken into account. Each layer should be rateable individually. At the same time, the rating of the related content layers shall influence the rating of the item that is currently looked at. Therefore, we suggested a rating across several content layers (MSM10a, MSM10b) as follows. The key to combine the rating of the several layers is a weighting of the subset values. The weighted mean (WM) rating of a content item is calculated by joining the arithmetic means (M) of all ratings for it and weighting them together with the means of the ratings for its related content items.

Equation 3.1 shows the calculation of the arithmetic mean of all ratings (R) for one single content item (CSinc), where p is the number of ratings per content item.

$$M_{CSin} = \frac{\sum\limits_{i=1}^{p} R_p}{p}$$
(3.1)

Equation 3.2 shows the calculation of the weighted mean for one content item layer (CLay). The weighting factor to combine the different arithmetic means calculated in formula 3.1, is the length of the content items (L). (n) is the number of content items per layer.

$$WM_{CLay} = \frac{\sum\limits_{i=1}^{n} L_{CSin_i} \cdot M_{CSin_i}}{\sum\limits_{i=1}^{n} L_{CSin_i}}$$
(3.2)

The final calculation of the weighted mean for one content item that takes into account all related content layers underneath and above is shown in equation 3.3. The weighting factor to combine the different layers is the ratio of the number of ratings of that layer (NoR) to the number of content items of that layer (NoC), whereas the number of layers (m) is also needed for the calculation. This was chosen to on the one hand consider how many ratings were given and on the other hand not to minimize the effect of upper layers which by nature have less content items that can be rated.

$$WM_{CSin} = \frac{\sum\limits_{i=1}^{m} \frac{NoR_{CLay_i}}{NoC_{CLay_i}} \cdot WM_{CLay_i}}{\sum\limits_{i=1}^{m} \frac{NoR_{CLay_i}}{NoC_{CLay_i}}}$$
(3.3)

Since this more complex rating calculation takes more time than a standard one, it is only computed once and an item is saved and stored in the database as *CombinedRate* (see class diagram in figure 3.3). Whenever an overview page of the e-lectures is displayed, the combined rating only needs to be read from the database.

Two advantages are expected by using the new rating algorithm. First, more exact results and second, the automatic calculation of ratings for superordinate content items in the different content layers and therefore more rating results are anticipated. This is necessary, because the engagement of the students in the rating is not very high. In order to utilize the rating for content filtering despite the lack of data, the calculation

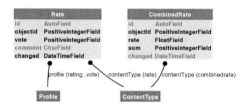

Figure 3.3: Class diagram of the rating module

over several layers automatically fills some data gap. Due to more user ratings being considered for one content item, when also taking related items into account, the rating gets more trustworthy even with a small data base. The next Web 2.0 function implemented is the community tagging, which will be explained in the next section.

3.1.2 A Pluggable Solution for Community Tagging

Collaborative tagging means that people have the role to assign keywords, which are called tags, to resources. Collaborative also means that all users in the community may agree to a tag a fellow user added and thereby rank it higher. Tags help to classify and summarize the content of a resource. (BBMB07), (GH05) The collection of all tags gathered that way is called folksonomy, even though the correctness of this term had been discussed (GH05). A folksonomy is formally defined as a quadruple $F :=$ (U, T, R, Y) whereby U, T and R are finite sets whose elements are users, tags and resources. Y represents the tag assignment, a relation between the three other sets, which can formally be described as $Y <= U x T x R$ (Nol10).

The tagging module in the tele-teaching environment was implemented in order to test to what extend it is used by the students. Some of the results presented in this section were previously published in (MSM11a). The class diagram of the tagging module (see figure 3.4) shows that the keyword of the tag itself is stored in the *TagText* class. This class is then associated to the *TagObject* class that stores which *TagText* is associated to which content item by which user. The *TagText* also references one of the languages in the portal. When using the possibility of enhancing keywords semantically within the tele-teaching portal (which will be explain in section 3.3.1), the other two classes *TagsConnection* and *ConnectionType* can be used to determine which tags are related to each other and what type of relation connects them.

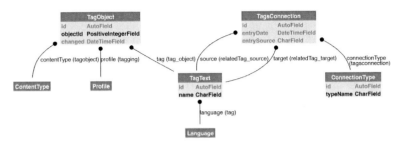

Figure 3.4: Class diagram of the tagging module

Two factors can ascertain the importance of a tag for a content item. The frequency with which the content item was tagged with a tag as well as the relevance of the tag for the content item are these two factors. One example: one lecture has 50 tags, where 'internet' is one of them. A second lecture only has 5 tags and *internet* is one of them. This tag is more relevant for the second lecture, because it is one of a very small amount of tags, whereas it is less relevant for the first lecture when it is one in a crowd. Figure 3.5 shows a visualization of two tags connected to four different learning objects. A connection is represented by an arrow. Multiple connections may exist between tags and objects, because a tag can be used several times with the same object when multiple users are involved. The importance of a tag is used for tag clouds on the one hand and for the use in recommendation algorithm on the other (see (SMM10a) for more explanation of the usage of tags for lecture video recommendation).

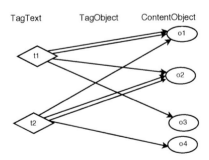

Figure 3.5: Relations between tags and content objects (MSM11a)

53

The tagging module has several interfaces attached (see figure 3.6). The first is the tag creation interface (see figure 3.6 middle right) which is appended to each of the three content layers (see the introduction of this chapter for further details). This interface includes a text field where the tag can be typed in. Auto-completion with existing tags in the portal is added to this textfield. Also, the language can be selected, because the portal is multi-lingual. Above this tag creation interface, existing tags are visualized. Own tags are marked with a 'my' icon whereas the other tags include a 'like'-icon, where one user can choose the same tag as another user without having to type it himself.

Figure 3.6: User interfaces for the tagging module

The second interface is the back-end interface (see figure 3.6 top left image), where the user can edit his own tags or quickly access the content items to these. A tag cloud (see figure 3.6 top right image) shows an overview of all tags in the portal. The size of them is determined by the number of usages in the portal. Clicking on any of these tags, the user will get an overview of all content items associated with this tag (see figure 3.6 bottom left image).

The learning process may be improved when utilizing tagging as well, for it helps making sense of the content that is consumed (GH05). In order to be able to select a tag, learners have to consume the content and reason about what they learned with it. This process supports them in participating actively in the learning instead of just

54

leaning back and passively consuming. With the help of tagging, the students actively analyse and process the content. Thereby they ascend in the taxonomy of learning to the level of 'application and analysis' (BBMB07), (Blo56). When even utilizing the tags to chose adjacent topics and browse superordinate and sub-ordinate topics, the highest level, which is 'synthesis and evaluation', can be reached (MSM11a). The students also benefit from the more accurate content description that follows tagging (BBMB07).

3.1.3 Personal Content Playlists

Personal content playlists in tele-teaching environments are typically used to collect content to a certain topic, to gather lectures needed for exam preparation or to provide the students with a collection of previous knowledge to a course (SMHM10). In the class diagram of the playlist module (see figure 3.7) one can see that a playlist is set up by a name, a description, a logo, some timestamps as well as the information if the playlist is public or not. Furthermore, the playlist is connected to a user profile of the user creating it. Within the playlist there may be several groups (*Playlist-Group*). Each group might have several content items (lectures or podcasts) included (this connection is represented by the Media class connected via *PlaylistEntry*).

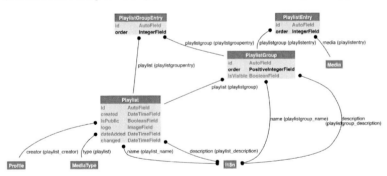

Figure 3.7: Class diagram of the playlist module

The playlist module has several interfaces that are rendered within the tele-teaching portal. First of all there is a playlists overview page (see figure 3.8 small image top left). On each lecture or podcast page, the interface to create a new playlist is shown (see figure 3.8 large background image). In this form, a dropdown box with all existing playlists of the currently logged in user is shown. They now have the option to select one of the lists or to create a new one. Then they only need to create a new group (as can also be seen in the before mentioned figure) or select an existing one in order to finalize adding the selected content item to the playlist. The playlist module is also intertwined with the RSS module. Users thereby have the option to subscribe to playlists of fellow users.

Figure 3.8: User interfaces for the playlist module

Because the playlist might be private or public, this parameter has to be considered when displaying a compilation of them. Listing 3.1 shows the Python code for retrieving all playlists of which the user has the rights to access from the database. If a user is logged in, all playlists with at least one element in them and where either the user is the creator or the public flag is set to true will be returned. If no user is logged in, only public playlists with at least one element will be displayed.

Listing 3.1: Django and Python Code to Collect Playlists for a View

```
1 if context["activeUser"]:
2 query = (Q(isPublic=True) & Q(number_elems__gt=0)) | Q(creator=c["activeUser"].
       profile)
3 playlists = Playlist.objects.annotate(numberElements=Count('playlistgroup__media')).
       filter(query).order_by('-changed')
4 else:
5 playlists = Playlist.objects.annotate(numberElements=Count('playlistgroup__media')).
       filter(isPublic=True, numberElements__gt=0).order_by('-changed')
```

3.1.4 Findings From the Implementation of Basic Web 2.0 Functions

Since 2009 those Web 2.0 functionalities have been implemented and researched in the sample tele-teaching portal. To summarize it, those Web 2.0 functions are tagging, rating, the creation of links to the content, user-generated playlists and simple user-generated time-based annotations (GSM11). Table 2.1 in paragraph 2.2.4 gave a quick overview of how entries for which community function in the portal were generated by how many users after 1 1/2 years. From the table of user activities it was apparent that the participation of users in the creation of additional data to the lecture recordings is very low.

One of the reasons that can be imagined is the purpose those classical Web 2.0 functions were designed for. This purpose is not e-learning or tele-teaching, but rather collaboration, information creation and quick as well as easy sharing across different people, spaces and times. Of course all these purposes play a role in tele-teaching as well. But in contrast to the general application of Web 2.0, the process of dealing with learning material may take longer and include deeper involvement, which those quick classical Web 2.0 functions implemented so far do not deliver.

Therefore a more e-learning related tool was selected for implementation and analysis next. This tools is video annotation (see section 2.2.4 for more details). It was adapted to the principles of the Web 2.0 in order to support the aspects of collaboration and community. This is desirable, because collaboration may support distance learning.

Since the platform design is most probably another cause for this lack of incentive for participation, the next section will also address this issue. The collaborative digital lecture manuscript function which follows design guidelines for a culture of participation will be introduced.

3.2 Lecture Video Annotation Functions

The work described in this section was previously published in (Gru13), (GYM13b), (GYM+13a), (GM12). Before going deeper into the implementation of e-lecture annotation functions, definitions of annotations shall be clarified. The digital e-lecture annotation functions can be divided in individual and group use cases. Two umpteen definitions are used for both of them. Second, this work differentiates between two sundry functions developed. These are the textual annotation feature called *manuscript* and the quick time marking function called *marker*. The manuscript function assists in writing digital notes that can be used as a manuscript. Quickly saving specific timestamps in the video and adding a predefined tag to it is assisted by the marker function.

The digital lecture video annotation is defined as a quadruple of the annotation text, the content item it is attached to, the timestamp of the specific point within the video the annotation is attached to and the user ID of the user who has written the annotation:

Def.1: A textual individual annotation is defined by a quadruple a = (T, C, TS, U), with T = annotation text, C = content item, e.g lecture, TS = timestamp within the content item and U = user annotating the lecture.

The textual annotation may contain any free text sentence. Opposed to that, the text in the marker function may only be selected from a predefined set of short texts. There are some short texts provided as choice by the system, but the users may also define their own short texts. For collaboration purposes, the annotation might be shared within a learning group. The definition for the collaborative annotation has to be adapted the following way:

Def.2: A textual group annotation is defined by a quadruple a = (T, C, TS, U, G), with T = annotation text, C = content item, TS = timestamp within the content item, U = user annotating the lecture and G = group the user shares his annotation with.

Now that the definition was presented, the use cases of the annotation functions will be elaborated. The section afterwards will deal with a data model for the collaborative manuscript function, followed by a description of the interface. Finally, options to combine the manuscript function with other portal functionality will be explicated.

3.2.1   Use Cases for Students

The lecture video annotation features are implemented for every podcast and lecture. The digital manuscript provides functionality to write time-based digital notes while watching e-lectures using a wiki-like environment. Those notes can form the basic structure for a manuscript that the students may use for learning and revision. After watching the lecture the users can still add on to that basic structure to complete their notes. Several use cases can be differentiated within the lecture video annotation features:

- private and public annotation

- individual and group annotation

- live and on demand annotation

As visualized in the activity diagram in fig. 3.9, these use cases can be combined variously.

Two use cases for this function differ in the time within the lecture recording process they are used at. First, the lecture recording may be used any time after the lecture originally took place. The lecture may be substituted by the e-lecture or replayed for learning and revision purposes. The manuscript interface is situated right underneath the video player which shows the lecture in order to allow simultaneous watching and note writing. The second use case is live streaming. The students may watch the broadcasted stream at any other place or just use the annotation interface while the lecture is in fact taking place. The link to the manuscript interface as well as the livestream are made accessible via a respective calendar. An overview of upcoming streams and recordings is also provided to the students by this calendar.

The second differentiation is made between individual and group annotations. The miscellaneous combinations of the use cases allow to have for instance live group

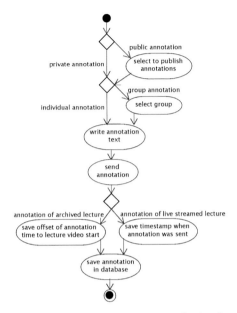

Figure 3.9: Activity diagram of the annotation function

annotations as well as public individual on demand annotations. One interface incorporates all those use cases in order to facilitate the usage for the students and to allow them a choice of different constellations in one spot. Solely the distinction between on demand and live annotations is undertaken by the system. The point of entry the user chooses determines which interface is used. If a lecture is selected from the video archive, an on demand annotation is created. When a live stream is selected via the live stream calendar, a live annotation will be created. Those two differ in their storage of the time, as will be explained in the next section.

3.2.2 A Data Model for Collaborative Creation of a Digital Lecture Manuscript

In the center of the data model is the class *Annotation* (see figure 3.11). This class holds the basic annotation parameters, like the text, a foreign key to the media item as well as the offset from the beginning of the media item. Furthermore a foreign key to the user who created the annotation, the language the annotation is written in, if it should be public or not and the creation dates, are stored.

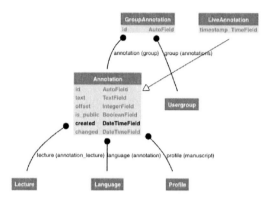

Figure 3.10: Class diagram of the manuscript function

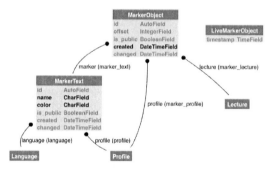

Figure 3.11: Class diagram of the marker function

In case the annotation is a collaborative note taking in a learning group, the class *GroupAnnotation* is the bridge between the class *Group* and the class *Annotation* that holds foreign keys to both and thereby stores the group annotations.

A comment might be written contemporaneously to a live lecture or a live streamed lecture or alternatively while watching an e-lecture on demand in the portal. In case of a live situation, the memo is stored in the class *LiveAnnotation*. Because the offset to the beginning of the lecture will not be available at this point, and also the lecture might be subject to further editing afterwards, the time of the remark within the e-lecture is not stored as offset, but as absolute timestamp.

The offset relative to the beginning of the lecture will only be calculated when the lecture is stored in the portal by the media department staff (see signal in listing 3.2).

Listing 3.2: Django and Python Code for an Event Sent When a Lecture is Saved.

```
1  lecture_start_changed = django.dispatch.Signal(providing_args=[' lecture', 'time', ])
2  [...]
3  if sendTimeEvent:
4          lecture_start_changed.send(sender=Lecture, lecture=self, time=self.startTime
                )
5  [...]
```

The objects in the *LiveAnnotation* class are thereby transformed to portal comments of the *Annotation* class. This is done by transforming the absolute timestamp of the memo into an offset and afterwards deleting the connected *LiveAnnotation* object (see listing 3.3). Although using the live note taking feature, students may nevertheless benefit from the video structuring and search capabilities of the notation feature at a later point, when the media file is actually buffered in the portal structure.

Listing 3.3: Django and Python code for transforming live in on demand annotations.

```
1  def after_lecture_start_changed_handler(sender, lecture, time = 0, **kwargs):
2      if time != 0:
3          liveannotations = LiveAnnotation.objects.filter(lecture = lecture)
4          for annotation in liveannotations:
5              annotation.offset = (datetime.combine(annotation.created, annotation.
                    timestamp) - datetime.combine(annotation.created, time)).seconds
6              annotation.save()
7              annotation.delete_liveannotation()
8
9  lecture_start_changed.connect(after_lecture_start_changed_handler, sender=Lecture,
        weak = False)
```

The same process of transforming the live use case into the portal use case is utilized for the markers. The absolute time is thereby transformed to an offset when the media file of the lecture recording is finally saved in the portal.

3.2.3 The User Interfaces

The user interfaces for the lecture video annotation functions are placed under the video player (see figure 3.12). The user interface on the top, directly underneath the player, is the form that allows entering time-based textual annotation functions. Second, the marker entering interface can be found. Third, the annotations that the user has already posted are rendered. At the bottom, the timeline with the users' markers is displayed. All the individual boxes can be open or closed, depending on the users' needs and preferences.

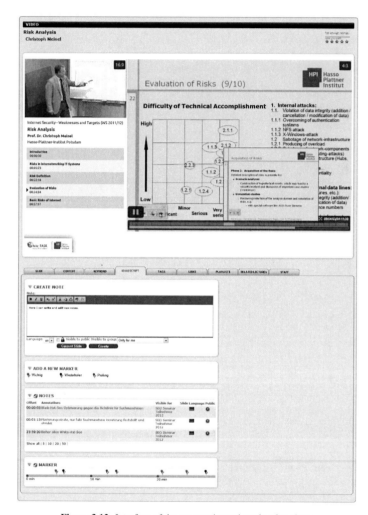

Figure 3.12: Interface of the manuscript and marker functions

Entering Textual Annotations to Lecture Videos

As preliminary tests have revealed that formatting possibilities are a major requirement to the users, the text-field is enhanced with a WYSIWYG-editor that allows visual editing of the notes. The final HTML code that, together with Javascript in the
back-end, enables instant editing of a text in supported HTML-classes, is shown in
listing 3.4. The text field itself is rendered as iframe with the body tag having the ID
"tinymce". Through this ID, the Javascript that performs the action of transforming
the text including the formatting applied to it to a storable format by transforming the
formatting signals into a set of special characters.

Listing 3.4: Final HTML code rendering the WYSIWYG-editor.

```
1   <table id="id_text_tbl" class="mceLayout" [...]>
2       <tbody>
3           <tr class="mceFirst">
4               <td class="mceToolbar mceLeft mceFirst mceLast">
5                   [...] // source code to render the WYSIWYG buttons
6               </td>
7           </tr>
8           <tr class="mceLast">
9               <td class="mceIframeContainer mceFirst mceLast">
10                  <iframe id="id_text_ifr" src='javascript:""' frameborder="0"
                        style="width: 100%; height:127px;">
11                      <html>
12                          <head>[...]</head>
13                          <body id="tinymce" class="mceContentBody "
                                spellcheck="false" dir="ltr"></body></
                                html>
14                  </iframe>
15              </td>
16          </tr>
17      </tbody>
18  </table>
```

The table of all annotations, which the user has posted so far to the current media
item, starts with the timestamp of the annotation. It can be used as a direct link into the
video. This is a most helpful use case for students who wish to repeat the lecture for
exam preparation or revision. The annotation text follows in the next column. Double-
clicking the annotation text will allow the user to edit the annotation text on the spot.
Deleting the annotation is also possible in the last column.

Marking Important Video Sections with Time Markers

The marker creation interface holds a number of visual markers. The system provides some pre-defined markers. Those can be defined in advance by the system administrators. They are available for all lectures. General terms like *exam preparation*,
revise or *question* can be chosen for repeating tasks. The users may also create own
markers by themselves, select a color and enter a keyword to them in the backend in-

terface. By only clicking those markers the user may now easily bookmark certain times in the video and tag them with most essential keywords.

The last interface is the timeline displaying all markers that a student has used to bookmark a certain timestamp in the lecture video. Again those markers can be used as direct link into the video. The markers are distributed on the timeline by using their timestamp to calculate their position (see listing A.1 in appendix).

Generating Screenshots from Lecture Videos for the Manuscript

From preliminary studies the usage of the visual slides was known to be important to the students while watching lecture videos. They give students visual hints which topic is dealt with where in the video. These visual hints are also interesting for the utilization of lecture video annotations, because they give the students an orientation within the 90 minutes of a lecture. In order not to overwhelm with those slides, the "current slide" button in the textual annotation creation interface can be used to select a screenshot at a certain point of time in the video and add it to their textual annotations making up a whole lecture manuscript afterwards.

3.2.4 Culture of Participation

The digital manuscript function can be utilized in either a single user or group mode. The group mode supports users in the same group to annotate the video at any point in time while at the same time seeing and later also editing each others' annotations. Students can create their own groups, for example together with peers from their learning group or other students in the same seminar or lecture. Lecturers may on the other hand also create groups and add their students to it. Because the students have to become active in order to make this collaborative learning setting successful, culture of participation principles shall be incorporated. Therefore five issues have to be tackled:

- Group awareness has to be fostered.

- Rewards from the group have to be incorporated.

- Scenarios to support problem-solving and online discussion have to be created.

- More students have to be engaged as coordinators and collaborators.

- Students have to be involved as meta-designers.

The use-case-diagram in figure 3.13 visualizes how group awareness can be fostered. These parts of the diagram that are marked in grey are those elements that should help to create a culture of participation. The first step therefore is to ensure that when a group of people is working at the same annotation, the authors are still obvious. A rights management system should make sure that annotations published within the group can really only be seen and edited by its members, that public annotations can be viewed by users outside off the group and that private annotations really stay private. This is necessary, because there exist those four types of the annotation - private, visible to the group and public and not linked to a group as well as public and linked to a group. An awareness function for instance is a statistic showing which users contributed which amount to the group. An update poll showing the latest contributions is a second awareness mechanism. Polling of all users' contributions to one group annotation interface as well as an overall "best user" statistic for the different Web 2.0 functions were implemented for this work .

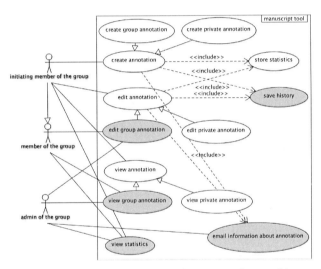

Figure 3.13: Highlights on participative elements in a use-case-diagram of the annotation function

Tracking the individual contributions can lead to a reward from the group. Also, the members of a group are aware that their input is being judged when a version control system is utilized. When notifications about the latest contributions are offered, the awareness for the participation of fellow learners is increased. A quantification of the participation of distinct group members is conciousness by counting all contributions and visualizing it in a statistic visible to each insider. Gamification features, like awarding an additional status or badge for well performing group members and also a voting system for very good group members, are further ways to implement reward.

To enable quick and easy low-level feedback, voting can be implemented on the annotation-level. A new research field has recently opened up on these last mentioned triggers for group awareness and reward: gamification, which was the topic of a number of research papers amongst which are for example (DDKN11), (BKTS13), (HK13). When it comes to grading the students or assessing a large number of students in an informal MOOC scenario, those mechanisms are a benefit for the teacher as well as especially the voting feedback by fellow students can be an indicator for valuable input. If participation is defined as a part of the learning targets, the statistics can be used as another input source for the student evaluation. Textual group feedback is a further help for grading.

When offering a flexible and open annotation system, problem-solving and online discussions could also be incorporated. Spreading some seeds to trigger these processes is a task that the teacher can take over as Reinhart et al. (REM11) explained. A possible scenario is when the tutor asks questions during the lecture. Using the digital annotation tool, the students may then be given the task to discuss these issues and document the process of controversy. When annotating a live lecture, students may even use the annotation tool to post questions themselves. The lecturer may then use one or more pre-defined time slots within or at the end of the session to answer these matters. There exist several systems that include the last mentioned type of question-answering during presentations or lectures that even enable voting and thereby also ranking of these queries, like SpeakUp [1] or embedded into speaker feedback systems like the Live Interest Meter (RPLZS13). The advantage of including this procedure in the annotation process is that the student may use one and the same interface for both purposes and does not need to switch systems while at the same time listening to the lecturer.

To engage more students as contributors and coordinators can have different facets. By forming their own groups and jointly writing their own manuscripts, students can for example use the annotation tool for their learning process and further discussion while at the same time becoming coordinators and collaborators themselves. On the other hand, the teacher can also create a learning group and open it up to a specific group of learners. A seminar setting, where students give talks to present different topics, is one possible use case. These presentations can be recorded. The annotation interface in the tele-teaching environment will be used for discussion and questioning by fellow learners in this case.

The last part in the culture of participation is meant to give learners the freedom to act as meta-designers. If the annotation environment itself is designed in a free and open manner, it already gives the learner this freedom. Then they have the opportunity

---

[1] http://doplab.unil.ch/speakup

to use the environment in a way suitable for their matters and their learning style and adapt it according to their needs. Already now it is possible to use structure and design besides simple textual annotations to some extent. Using full wiki-like function would enable even more editing and include the possibility to upload the users' own files. One use case of the students for the annotation environment is the collaborative creation of a lecture manuscript including slide images and structured textual annotations. This manuscript could then be used for exam preparation, as later point of entry for further learning and research or simply as a summary of the topic.

Especially the issue of the extended research can even be enhanced by using further tools and combining the manuscript function with other functions in the tele-teaching portal. The next section will go deeper into this topic.

3.2.5   Combining the Manuscript with Other Portal Functions

There are several possibilities to combine the digital manuscript tool with other portal functions. Playlists, PDF export and the search are examples that will be elaborated in this section.

PDF Export of the Digital Manuscipt

When the users have created the digital version of the lecture manuscript by writing individual notes, they may utilize these notes digitally in order to re-visit certain points in time of the lecture. Moreover, in preliminary studies, we found out that students still like to have a hard-copy of their notes for learning purposes. In result, a PDF export option was developed for the manuscript. The PDF export includes written notes as well as screenshots of the slides the user inserted manually.

Combining the Digial Manuscript with Playlists

Lecture video playlists (see section 3.1.3) can be used to collect which lecture videos they want to see next. After they have seen all these videos and made annotations to them, it again might be helpful to offer a PDF export of all the annotations a student created for the specific theme of the playlist (for instance the topics of a whole semester, a certain topic in the subject etc.). In order to facilitate this export for all videos in the playlist, a PDF export is offered for all those lectures at once.

Using User-Generated Notes for Searching

In the introduction, it was motivated that a solid metadata base was very important for the search process in multimedia data, because this data in itself is not easily searchable. In section 2.3 all possible metadata sources, including administrative, automatically harvested and user-generated metadata were listed. User notes, that were produced with the help of the manuscript function, belong to the user-generated metadata and are hence a valuable asset for the search function of the portal.

Figure 3.14: Video search via the manuscript function - global search (left) and search amongst users' own notes (right)

This is the case as the user annotations may help to resolve keyword search requests to a certain point in time within the video. Users annotations are time-bound and specific keywords might be extracted from them. Matching those keywords with keywords in a query will thus result in allocating the search key phrases to specific points in time within the video. The search for annotations was included in the global portal search of the sample tele-teaching web portal.

Figure 3.14 shows the user interfaces for the two types of annotation search the users can perform. On the one hand, they can use the global portal search and thus also query all publicly available user annotations for the keyterm they are looking for (see image on the left hand side in the figure). On the other hand they may also search among their own notes (see image on the right hand side in the figure) and thereby retrieve their previously created annotations including a link into the video at exactly the position the note was created at.

To leave more choice to the user, he can decide between different search types, which are a case-sensitive (exact) or case-insensitive exact match (iexact) or a case-sensitive (contains) or case-insensitive containment test (icontains). With the search type decided, the search term will then be queried against all annotations for this authorization level (user only or public).

The search function is the first utilizing keyword information from the manuscript by querying key terms against it. It is also possible to extract keywords from the annotation using keyword detection algorithms or the semantic web. The user-generated data is unstructured information. For the sake of search and filtering, this is no feasible pre-requisite, since it is not machine readable and not easily processable. Hence, transferring this social data into structured or semi-structured data is a prerequisite to efficiently integrate this data into search and filtering algorithms. An extraction process which takes keywords from user-generated data and maps them into a semantic context, will be introduced in the next section.

3.3   A Semantic Topic Map

When thinking about visualizations for the semantic context of a keyword, one comes to deliberate on how collections of similar topics are visualized. Due to their popularity, tag clouds are a first visualization to come into ones mind. Using tag clouds only allows showing a prioritization between the different words, this is why connections between them words are not shown. Second, topic maps immediately come into the focus of the thoughts. This is the case, because topic maps are able to visualize connections between topics and are often used to provide an overview of a topic and its sub-fields as well as related themes. Talking about semantic connections, the relations can also be both sub-topics, related topics and parent-topics in addition. Figure 3.15 shows the difference between tag clouds and topic maps. Both visualize some of the topics presented in the abstract of this thesis as an example. In the tag cloud one can immediately see which of the keywords are most prominent whereas in the topic map the connections between the individual themes become visible.

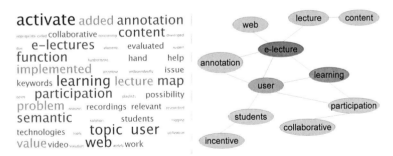

Figure 3.15: Tag cloud versus topic map

When the method of visualization is selected, the data needs to be generated. A first algorithm to generate this data was developed utilizing existing keywords in the tele-teaching portal. The first section in this chapter will introduce this primary algorithm. It extracts related terms to a keyword from a Semantic Web data repository. It does not include a ranking of those terms, though. Furthermore, only predefined key terms can be used. Keyword identification within running text, like for example from user-generated annotations, is not possible. But exactly the connection between user-generated annotations and Semantic Web networks is desired within the scope of this thesis, as was motivated in section 2.3.2. Therefore, a second more sophisticated algorithm is utilized. It on the one side allows running text as input and on the other side produces ranked keyword lists as output. Employing different existing algorithms for semantic entity mapping, neighbour discovery and ranking in connection with the DBpedia dataset allows to automatically generate semantic topic maps. Related work and technology decisions of this procedure, which is applied in the approach that will be described in the second section of this chapter, are explained in section 2.3.2.

3.3.1   A Basic Method to Retrieve Semantic Data from Keywords

The basic method of retrieving semantic data from keywords builds on the idea that different modules in a tele-teaching portal, like the search module and the tagging module, already produced and will continuously keep on producing keywords which might be the starting point to retrieve a semantic context. Hence, this newly build module can be triggered by different other modules in the portal and their keywords (see figure 2.7 (MSM11b) and subsection 2.3.1 for more details). The input keywords might on the one hand be derived from a folksonomy, for example when it came from the tagging module. On the other hand it may originate from automatically generated keywords, for instance when being provided by the OCR module that extracts textual information from the video track of the lecture.

In this first basic algorithm, no real named entity recognition and disambiguation as well as entity mapping takes place. We rather utilize the information that is implicitly hidden in the URI. Each entity is identified by a unique uniform resource identifier (URI), which is presented in the form *http://DBpedia.org/resource/Keyword* (BKLI07). The very basic mapping procedure only appends the keyword input by the module to the first part of the URI *http://DBpedia.org/resource/* and thereby tries out if a matching entity existed.

Looking at how contextual information in DBpedia can be retrieved, it was found that two different types of relations are of interest. These are synonyms and generalization. The generalization is interesting in parent relations as well as in child relations. There are three predicate types in the Semantic Web that support us in the retrieval of the before mentioned groups of relations. The redirect is an indicator for synonyms. Subject and broader are signs for a term generalization. Being included in a triple of *Subject-Predicate-Object*, these attribute types include references to other related DBpedia entities like synonyms and categories, which can be regarded as related entities to the start entity (MSM11b).

Figure 3.16 explicates the proposed algorithm.

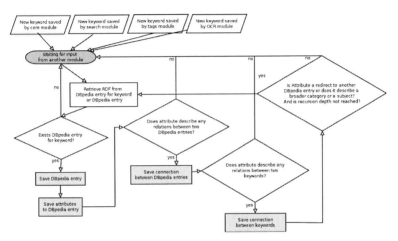

Figure 3.16: Basic workflow of the extraction of semantic relations to keywords in the portal (MSM11b)

The algorithm furthermore includes the transfer from the semantic world back to the portal. Whenever a connection between two semantic entities is discovered, it will be looked at as if there were two matching keywords in the portal. If so, a relation between those would also be saved in the database. Also included is a recursion, which will always go one step further each time a connection between the start entity and a neighbour entity is discovered.

If the recursion depth is not reached yet, neighbours to that neighbour entity will be retrieved as well. This idea of a recursion to gather larger relation maps over several steps and the idea of matching relations back to the portal are also being utilized in the second more sophisticated extraction algorithm (see figure 3.17 as an example for the recursion of the advanced algorithm visualized in a topic map), which will be introduced in the next section.

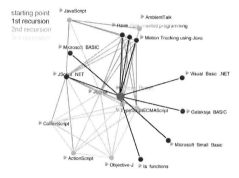

Figure 3.17: Example of the recursion in the semantic context retrieval algorithm

3.3.2 Utilizing User-Generated Annotations to Implement a Semantic Topic Map

In order to utilize the user-generated annotation data to retrieve the semantic context, the first step ist the recognition of DBpedia entities out of the annotations. In order to do so, several steps have to be gone through. The named entity recognition is the first step. Afterwards follow disambiguation and entity linking. When the relevant entities are extracted from the annotation, related entities to those have to be retrieved. This step is followed by a ranking of those neighbour entities to determine the most interesting ones. This results in a list of related entities and their distance to each other. The best ranked matches can then be utilized for the display in a semantic topic map. In this section, the different steps of this semantic extraction process, which is visualized in figure 3.18, will be explicated. All of these steps were implemented in one workflow, in order to retrieve a semantic context to the user's annotations and finally be able to display this context to the user. The motivation as well as major decisions concerning algorithms and tools to use for the semantic extraction process were explicated in section 2.3.2. Therefore this section will focus directly on the implementation.

Determining Semantic Entities in User-generated Annotations

Linking semantic entities to the user-generated annotations is the first step for utilizing Linked Open Data. For this task, Mendez wrote a service in 2011 (MJGSB11). Because of the decision to use DBpedia as dataset in the Linked Open Data initiative, utilizing also this service, called DBpedia Spotlight, that directly connects unstructured data to DBpedia, is the choice for this work. Also, the evaluation of the DBpedia

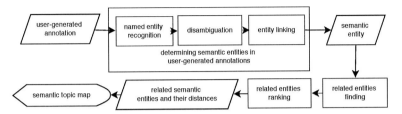

Figure 3.18: Workflow of the semantic extraction process gathering the topic map data

algorithm revealed quite good results in comparison with similar systems (RT11) having high precision rates with relatively low recall (MJGSB11). Another advantage are the configuration options that allow the user to determine the precision-recall-tradeoff according to the requirements of the application.

The DBpedia Spotlight service returns a list of entities that have been identified in the text lines inserted for entity detection. It is offered as a web service that can be called using the text that should be annotated as a parameter as shown in listing 3.5. Next to the entities, the return values also include two parameters measuring how connected the entity was to the text that was inserted. Those two parameters are resource prominence and disambiguation confidence.

Listing 3.5: Python code to call the spotlight service.

```
1   url = 'http://spotlight.DBpedia.org/rest/annotate'
2   data = {'confidence': configured_spotlight_confidence, 'support':
        configured_sportlight_support, 'text': user_generated_annotation}
3   headers = {'accept': 'application/json'}
4
5   try:
6       response = requests.post(url, data=data, headers=headers)
7   except (requests.exceptions.RequestException, requests.exceptions.HTTPError):
8       raise SpotlightError
```

The resource prominence determines how common the identified entity was whereas the disambiguation confidence was a factor from 0 to 1 showing how likely it is that the entity belongs to the keyword. Those two factors could also be handed to the web service as parameters in order only to return results within a desired range of values. The support parameter in listing 3.5 is the resource prominence and the confidence parameter is the disambiguation confidence. The disambiguation confidence takes the topical pertinence (relevance of the annotated resource for the context) and the contextual ambiguity (if there were several possible candidates) into account. Precision and recall as well as the level of annotation are therefore configurable and are a trade-off between the number of the desired results and the quality of the results (W3C11). For example, requesting a confidence of 0.7 would result in 70% of the wrong results having a topical pertinence threshold below the calculated one and would hence be eliminated. At the same time, the contextual ambiguity would have to be less than (1 - confidence), which is 0.3. The lower the ambiguity the higher the chance that the correct entities are annotated, but the higher also the chance that some correct entities are not annotated (MJGSB11).

The type of the return value can be selected, the JSON result is returned like in the example shown in listing 3.6, too.

Listing 3.6: JSON data returned from the DBpedia Spotlight service.

```
1  {u'@confidence': u'0.2', u'@sparql': u'', u'@support': u'20', u'@text': u'World Wide
      Web', u'@policy': u'whitelist', u'@types': u'', u'Resources': [{u'@support': u'
      2013', u'@URI': u'http://DBpedia.org/resource/World_Wide_Web', u'@surfaceForm': u
      'World Wide Web', u'@offset': u'0', u'@percentageOfSecondRank': u'-1.0', u'
      @similarityScore': u'0.3006775975227356', u'@types': u'Freebase:/visual_art/
      visual_art_medium,Freebase:/visual_art,Freebase:/law/invention,Freebase:/law,
      Freebase:/computer/protocol_provider,Freebase:/computer,Freebase:/cvg/
      cvg_platform,Freebase:/cvg,Freebase:/location/location,Freebase:/location,DBpedia
      :TopicalConcept'}]}
2  annotation success: {'keywords': [(u'http://DBpedia.org/resource/World_Wide_Web', u'
      World Wide Web')], 'success': True}
```

The second step on the way to gather the semantic context to the keyword is the search for related entities, which will be described in detail in the next paragraph.

Related Entities Finding

The search for related entities is processed within the semantic dataset DBpedia on the one hand and within the context of the start entity on the other. A combination of different neighbour search functions is therefore used. The decision was made to search for neighbours with a broad variety of algorithms, because there are many different reasons why entities might be related (see section 2.3.2 for a detailed overview and related work). Furthermore, due to the wide variety of possible topics, the diverse neighbour search algorithms might be differently successful depending on the start entity. Therefore all algorithms introduced in this paragraph are used in the final prototype. A ranking of all neighbours will finally determine the quality of the neighbours based on their proximity. A summary of the whole neighbour discovery workflow, where all the individual neighbour discovery algorithms are processed one after the other, and the results are collected in one big list, is visualized in figure 3.19. This paragraph will go though all the algorithms in detail.

For those neighbour discovery algorithms that take advantage of the DBPedia dataset, access to this repository is required. DBpedia offers the possibility to download the whole database and run one's own offline version, but it also supplies an online SPARQL-endpoint where the database can be queried online. The second option is chosen, because the aim is to discover whether standard semantic web technologies can serve as data provider for semantic topic maps or not. For this goal, only small

Figure 3.19: Activity diagramm of neighbour entity finding

amounts of data needed to be crawled for test purposes and an own dedicated database would have created too much overhead for that purpose.

Finding Neighbours Via the Annotation Text

Already in the disambiguation process, the context of the linked key term was important to determine which entity was linked to the keyword. Now again the context can give valuable information to find related entities to a keyword. Looking at the following possible annotation from a student: "In the internet HTML, Javascript as well as PHP are well-known programming languages for web applications." the term internet (URI: http://DBpedia.org/resource/Internet) is identified as the first semantic entity. The following entities that would be identified by DBpedia Spotlight: *HTML, Javascript, PHP, programming language* and *web application*, are very likely proper candidates for related entities to internet. On these grounds, all entities retrieved by DBpedia Spotlight from one and the same annotation, are considered for the neighbour ranking.

Finding Neighbours Via the Entity's Abstact

The same type of related entities finding can be processed with the abstract of the entity. When Wikipedia articles are transformed for the use in DBpedia, one of the attributes created is the abstract text of the article. Again, the description of the item might reveal relevant related items and is therefore used in the related entity finding process of this work. Looking at the first sentences in the abstract of the term Internet, the human user could already identify at least six potential neighbours that are emphasized in figure 3.20. The abstract of the start entity is thus inserted into DBpedia Spotlight. All entities found in the abstract are regarded as possible neighbours for the neighbour ranking.

Finding Entities by Following Categories

The next option is to find neighbours that share one or more categories with the entity within the DBpedia (NMO[+]). In order to find this out, all categories of the item have

The **Internet** is a global system of interconnected **computer networks** that use the standard **Internet protocol** suite (**TCP/IP**) to serve billions of users worldwide. It is a network of networks that consists of millions of private, public, academic, business, and government networks, of local to global scope, that are linked by a broad array of electronic, wireless and optical networking technologies. The Internet carries an extensive range of information resources and services, such as the inter-linked **hypertext** documents of the **World Wide Web** (WWW) and the infrastructure to support **email**.

Figure 3.20: Beginning of the abstract of the term *internet* in DBpedia

to be retrieved from DBpedia with the help of the query language SPARQL first. The size of the category, which denotes the number of entities that belong to that category, is extracted as well. This is necessary, because very large categories, like for example $http://DBpedia.org/page/Category : Living\_people$, are not very helpful, since they are just too broad and so the results would consequently be too unprecise. Some entities are part of very large categories and have a lot of categories, which would result in thousands of neighbours to rank, which is a performance issue. This is not a desired goal for a topic map, since the number of results that can be displayed is limited and thus only the closest items should be included. Therefore large categories (in this work a category with more than 55 entities was defined a large category, but further research needs to be conducted to determine which number should be used) are excluded.

Once the categories have been found, the other entities in those categories are extracted.

Finding Neighbours by Exploring Entities with the Same Type

The next method of finding neighbours is exploring the semantic connection type *rdf:type* within the DBpedia dataset (NMO^+). This type is a sort of category that includes entities of the same type. For instance, the entity $http://DBpedia.org/resource/JavaScript$ has 19 different types, amongst which are $DBpedia - owl : ProgrammingLanguage$ and $yago : ScriptingLanguages$. The scripting languages type is referenced by 176 entities that are potential neighbour candidates for the JavaScript programming language, for example $DBpedia : PHP$, $DBpedia : Perl$, $DBpedia : Python_{(programming_language)}$ and $DBpedia : Ruby_{(programming_language)}$ (see figure 3.21). Through those connections, potential neighbour candidates can be gathered.

Again very large type categories are not selected, because the entities connectedness computation would otherwise take too long. Also the number of neighbour entities chosen will be limited again for the same reasons as with the standard cate-

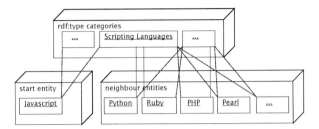

Figure 3.21: Example of neighbour retrieval by the category rdf:type

gory. Toward that target, first of all the rdf:type 'categories' of the number of entities referencing them are queried (see listing 3.7) and the resulting categories filtered.

Listing 3.7: SPARQL query for the type groups of an entity.

```
1  SELECT DISTINCT ?t AS ?type, count(?n) AS ?size
2  WHERE {<%(entity)s> rdf:type ?t. ?n rdf:type ?t.}
```

Afterwards, again all entities within those type categories are retrieved with the help of a SPARQL statement as shown in listing 3.8. Those are also added to the list of related entities of the start entity.

Listing 3.8: SPARQL to get the entities within the type groups.

```
1  SELECT ?e, COUNT(?p) AS ?c WHERE {?e rdf:type <%(type)s>. ?e [] ?p.} order by ?c
```

Finding Neighbours Via Direct Reference

A further method of retrieving neighbours follows the direct references from the start entity to neighbours within the DBpedia graph (NMO^+). For example the resource *Javascript* directly references the two resources $http : //dbpedia.org/resource/Mozilla_{Foundation}$ and $http : //dbpedia.org/resource/Netscape$ via the predicate $dbpprop : developer$. Also the entity of the scripting language ActionScript would be found as one result when following the direct reference with the predicate $DBpedia - owl : influencedBy$.

Listing 3.9: SPARQL query for direct reference neighbours.

```
1  SELECT ?o WHERE {{<%(entity)s> [] ?o.} UNION {?o [] <%(entity)s>}}
```

After the directly referenced neighbours have been retrieved from DBpedia by the SPARQL query, they have to be filtered again. Only if they are direct references within DBpedia they will be considered as related entities. Just the entities within DBpedia can be included in the ranking algorithm, because their position within the large entity graph is known. By finding the string "$http$: $//dbpedia.org/$" as part of the value text, it can be determined if an entity belongs to the DBpedia.

After all possible neighbour entities are retrieved, they ought to be ranked in order to select the best choice for the display in the semantic topic map. The following paragraph will explicate this in more details.

Related Entities Ranking

There are two algorithms used for the ranking (see figure 3.22). The first one utilizes all categories of the start entity with all neighbours that can be detected via the categories. This algorithm works with the degrees of the entities (see section 2.3.2 for a definition of the degree) and the log distance of these degrees (MST11). The second algorithm can be used for all other neighbours. It applies the vector space model (SWY75), builds predicate vectors for each of the entities as well as the start entity (NMO[+], GM07, Men13). By calculating the cosine similarity of each of the neighbours' vectors with the vector of the start entity, the relatedness can be computed (NMO[+], GM07, Men13).

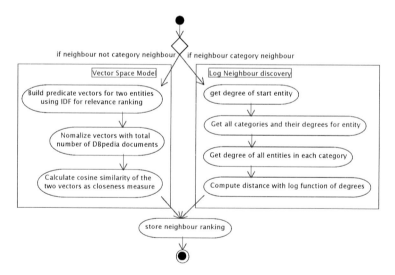

Figure 3.22: Activity diagramm of neighbour entity ranking

Entities Ranking by Following Categories

The first algorithm using the category data starts with getting the degree of the start entity (see listing 3.10). The degree of an entity is the number of its categories.

Listing 3.10: SPARQL query to get the degree of an entity.

```
1   select count(?category) as ?startEntityDegree where {
2        <%(entity)s> dcterms:subject ?category
3        }
```

The second step is querying the categories of the start entity and their degrees (see listing 3.11). The degree of a category is the number of its entities.

Listing 3.11: SPARQL query to get all categories of an entity including their degree.

```
1   select count(?categoryEntity) as ?categoryDegree ?categories where {
2        <%(entity)s> dcterms:subject ?categories.
3        ?categoryEntity dcterms:subject ?category.
4        }
```

The third step is getting all entities of the categories that were just retrieved and also querying their degrees (see listing 3.12). Counting the number of categories that belong to the entities is again the method to determine the degree of the entities.

Listing 3.12: SPARQL query to retrieve neighbour entities and their degrees within a category.

```
1        select ?subject count(?object) as ?entityDegree where
2        {
3             ?subject dcterms:subject <%(category)s>.
4             ?subject dcterms:subject ?object
5        } order by ?count
```

When all this data was gathered, the final calculation of the costs of following the connection from the start entity via the categories to neighbour entities has to be processed. This is done by summing up the logarithms of the degrees retrieved from DBpedia according to the following formula:

$$distance = distance_{\text{startEntityToCategory}} + distance_{\text{categoryToNeighbourEntity}} \qquad (3.4)$$

$$distance_{\text{startEntityToCategory}} = log(degree(startEntity)) + log(degree(category)) \qquad (3.5)$$

$$distance_{\text{categoryToNeighbourEntity}} = log(degree(category)) + log(degree(neighbourEntity)) \qquad (3.6)$$

Entities Ranking with the Vector Space Model

In order to utilize the vector space model and process each entity as a vector, the relevance of its predicates has to be detected for the use as vector data. Looking at all the rdf-triples, the relevance calculation for the predicates will be done in such form for which all predicates will be taken into account where the entity is either the subject or the object.

At the beginning, all the predicates for the start entity and the neighbour entities are retrieved with the help of the following SPARQL statement, listed in 3.13.

Listing 3.13: SPARQL query to get predicates from entity.

```
1   select ?predicate where {
2          <%(entity)s> ?predicate [].
3      }
```

When all predicates have been assembled in a list, the number of occurrences for each of them is calculated so as to be able to process the relevance ranking afterwards. The SPARQL statement in listing 3.14 is used to process this calculation.

Listing 3.14: SPARQL query to the occurrences of a predicate.

```
1   select count(distinct ?s) as ?count where {
2          ?s <%(predicate)s> [].
3      }
```

Typically TF/IDF or IDF calculations (SM83) can be used to resolve the relevance of a term in a document accumulation. In a preliminary study, it should be determined which of those two algorithms worked better for the purpose of ranking data for the use in semantic topic maps. In result, a fixed set of DBpedia entities was determined and ranked with the help of TF/IDF and IDF. Figure 3.23 shows the results of this preliminary test. Both of them came out with quite similar results in terms of the top ranked findings. But the threshold between desired (marked in green) and undesired (marked in red) effects is much more visible in the IDF only version due to the greater gap between the distance values of the desired and undesired results. Thus, IDF was chosen for the application in the semantic topic map.

The term frequency $tf(t, d)$ is defined as number of occurences of the term t in the document d. The document frequency $df(t, D)$ is defined as the number of documents in a set D, which includes the term t. Transferring this to our domain, the document frequency $df(p, D)$ is the number of triples t in our set DBpedia DBP, which includes the predicate p (see formula 3.7). The IDF value of each predicate p of an entity can be calculated considering the document frequency df and the total number of documents in the domain DBP. Formula 3.8 shows the calculation of the inverse document frequency for each of the predicates:

$$df(p, DBP) = |t \in DBP : p \in t| \tag{3.7}$$

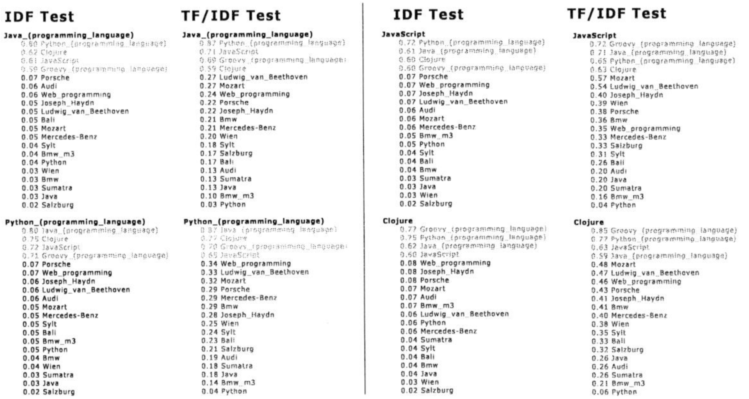

IDF Test

Java_(programming_language)
0.60 Python_(programming_language)
0.62 Clojure
0.61 JavaScript
0.58 Groovy_(programming_language)
0.07 Porsche
0.06 Audi
0.06 Web_programming
0.05 Joseph_Haydn
0.05 Bali
0.05 Mozart
0.05 Mercedes-Benz
0.04 Bmw_m3
0.04 Python
0.03 Wien
0.03 Bmw
0.03 Sumatra
0.03 Java
0.02 Salzburg

Python_(programming_language)
0.80 Java_(programming_language)
0.75 Clojure
0.72 JavaScript
0.75 Groovy_(programming_language)
0.07 Porsche
0.07 Web_programming
0.06 Ludwig_van_Beethoven
0.06 Joseph_Haydn
0.06 Audi
0.05 Mozart
0.05 Mercedes-Benz
0.05 Sylt
0.05 Bali
0.05 Python
0.04 Bmw
0.04 Wien
0.03 Sumatra
0.03 Java
0.02 Salzburg

TF/IDF Test

Java_(programming_language)
0.87 Python_(programming_language)
0.71 JavaScript
0.68 Groovy_(programming_language)
0.59 Clojure
0.27 Ludwig_van_Beethoven
0.27 Mozart
0.24 Web_programming
0.22 Porsche
0.22 Joseph_Haydn
0.21 Bmw
0.20 Wien
0.18 Sylt
0.17 Salzburg
0.17 Bali
0.13 Audi
0.13 Sumatra
0.13 Java
0.10 Bmw_m3
0.03 Python

Python_(programming_language)
0.87 Java_(programming_language)
0.77 Clojure
0.70 Groovy_(programming_language)
0.65 JavaScript
0.34 Web_programming
0.33 Ludwig_van_Beethoven
0.32 Mozart
0.29 Porsche
0.29 Mercedes-Benz
0.29 Bmw
0.28 Joseph_Haydn
0.25 Wien
0.24 Sylt
0.21 Salzburg
0.19 Audi
0.18 Sumatra
0.16 Java
0.14 Bmw_m3
0.04 Python

IDF Test

JavaScript
0.72 Python_(programming_language)
0.61 Java_(programming_language)
0.60 Clojure
0.60 Groovy_(programming_language)
0.07 Porsche
0.07 Web_programming
0.07 Joseph_Haydn
0.07 Ludwig_van_Beethoven
0.06 Audi
0.06 Mozart
0.05 Bmw_m3
0.05 Python
0.04 Sylt
0.04 Bali
0.03 Sumatra
0.03 Java
0.02 Salzburg

Clojure
0.77 Groovy_(programming_language)
0.75 Python_(programming_language)
0.62 Java_(programming_language)
0.60 JavaScript
0.08 Web_programming
0.08 Joseph_Haydn
0.08 Mozart
0.07 Audi
0.07 Bmw_m3
0.06 Ludwig_van_Beethoven
0.06 Python
0.06 Mercedes-Benz
0.04 Sumatra
0.04 Java
0.04 Bali
0.04 Java
0.03 Wien
0.02 Salzburg

TF/IDF Test

JavaScript
0.72 Groovy_(programming_language)
0.71 Java_(programming_language)
0.65 Python_(programming_language)
0.63 Clojure
0.57 Mozart
0.54 Ludwig_van_Beethoven
0.40 Joseph_Haydn
0.39 Wien
0.38 Porsche
0.36 Bmw
0.35 Web_programming
0.33 Mercedes-Benz
0.33 Salzburg
0.31 Sylt
0.26 Bali
0.20 Audi
0.20 Sumatra
0.16 Bmw_m3
0.04 Python

Clojure
0.85 Groovy_(programming_language)
0.77 Python_(programming_language)
0.59 Java_(programming_language)
0.48 Mozart
0.47 Ludwig_van_Beethoven
0.46 Web_programming
0.43 Porsche
0.43 Joseph_Haydn
0.41 Bmw
0.40 Mercedes-Benz
0.38 Wien
0.35 Sylt
0.33 Bali
0.32 Salzburg
0.26 Java
0.26 Audi
0.26 Sumatra
0.21 Bmw_m3
0.06 Python

Figure 3.23: Example comparison of the performance of TF/IDF versus IDF

$$idf(p, DBP) = log \cdot \frac{|DBP|}{df(p, DBP)} \tag{3.8}$$

Now, all the IDF values for the predicates that are in a relation to the entity the vector is built for, will be added to this vector of the entity. When all the vectors have been built, they will be normalized with the total number of documents in the DBpedia (the implementation worked with 33718937, a number retrieved in the middle of 2013) and the cosine similarity measure between the start entity's vector and the neighbour entity's vectors will determine the similarity between the entity and its neighbours. The cosine similarity can be calculated according to the following formula 3.9:

$$sim(vec_a, vec_b) = \frac{vec_a * vec_b}{|vec_a| * |vec_b|} \tag{3.9}$$

When all neighbour entities and their similarity value compared to the target entity are retrieved, the data can be stored for a later use in the semantic topic map. The next section will go into detail about this.

81

From the Extracted Data to the Topic Map Interface

Once the data is retrieved with the help of semantic web methods, it needs to be stored in the database and later on retrieved from it again to be handed over to the template that finally renders the topic map.

With the help of the class diagram in figure 3.24, one can see that the extracted keyword is separated from the semantic entity. The *AnnotationKeyword* class describes the actual keywords extracted from the user's notes. Therefore they include a key-term, a foreign to a specific annotation in a specific lecture and a foreign key to a semantic entity that could be matched to this keyword. Because the DBpedia Spotlight service is used for the detection of the keyword within the annotation and the term in the semantic entity returned from DBpedia Spotlight is not always equal to the keyword in the annotation, the exact key term within the notes needs to be saved for further processing.

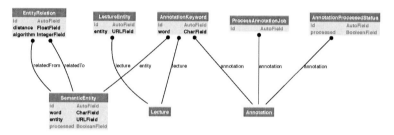

Figure 3.24: Class diagram of the topic map module

The *SemanticEntity* class then contains the DBpedia URI of the entity to uniquely identify it within the Semantic Web. The keyword contained in the URI is the second element of the entity, because it is needed for the visualization in the topic map. The processed flag is also utilized for the semantic topic map. If an entity was already processed, it can be used for further navigation within a network of topic maps. The user thereby has the chance to click through several topic maps until he finds the context he was interested in. The *EntityRelation* class finally stores the relations between the different entities with foreign keys on a source and a target entity as well as value determining how closely related the two entities are to each other.

The *LectureEntity* class maps one lecture to each of the entities. At the moment this is a manual process, which should be automatized later on. In order to insert these connections independent from the extraction of the semantic context of the entities, the entity in the *LectureEntity* class is not a foreign key, but uniquely identifies the entity by its URI. The classes *ProcessAnnotationJob* and *AnnotationProcessedStatus* are used to build a job queue for the semantic extraction processing. This is necessary to balance the load on the server.

The amount of extractable data from DBPedia could be too large to visualize. On account of this, some limitation of it will be necessary to be able to visualize this data in a topic map. Experiments by the author showed that for a standard laptop screen with the data that should be visualized in this work's topic map, 10 related items to the central keyword (5, 10, 15 and 20 items were tried) and a recursion depth of 2 (a recursion depth up to 5 was tried) with the amount of related items divided by the iteration cycle, are numbers that still allow a proper overview within the map. Those related items are the top ranked ones that result from the previously explained entity ranking algorithm.

On order to use a standardized data transport format, the Django internal data structure is converted to JSON to send it to the template. Calling the data retrieval from the template works via an AJAX request. Listing 3.15 shows the json structure for two links that will be displayed in the topic map.

Listing 3.15: JSON with topic map data returned to topic map template.

```
1  [{ "source": "JavaScript",
2        "targetProcessed": false,
3        "sourceURL": "http://DBpedia.org/resource/JavaScript",
4        "target": "Ruby_(programming_language)",
5        "sourceProcessed": true,
6        "targetURL": "http://DBpedia.org/resource/Ruby_(programming_language)",
7        "sourceLecture": 7191,
8        "targetLecture": 5967,
9        "value": 0.71013726523199705},
10 { "source": "SQL",
11       "targetProcessed": false,
12       "sourceURL": "http://DBpedia.org/resource/SQL",
13       "target": "Ruby_(programming_language)",
14       "sourceProcessed": true,
15       "targetURL": "http://DBpedia.org/resource/Ruby_(programming_language)",
16       "sourceLecture": 4957,
17       "targetLecture": 5967,
18       "value": 0.89611193785268195},...]
```

Included in one link item are the source and the target node, the DBpedia URLs of both nodes, the text of the keyword, the best lectures that can be associated to these terms, a boolean indicating whether the DBpedia entities were already processed, meaning if their semantic context was already extracted, as well as the value between 0 and 1 determining how close those two keywords are to each other.

When the data is transferred from the view to the template, the semantic topic map will be ready to be rendered. This part of the process is explained in the next section.

Semantic Topic Map Interface

Since the topic map is targeted for the tele-TASK web portal, the topic map solution had to be web-based as well. As the statistics of the tele-TASK portal showed that the users come from all kinds of devices and platforms, the solution had to be independent of the platform used. Therefore, the back-end for the semantic topic map is implemented in a combination of Python with Django in connection with HTML, SVG and Javascript in the front-end. This method was chosen because SVG can be rendered without additional plugins by the major browsers and supports the platform independence as well as device independence. To ease the process of development and to improve the support for different browsers, a high-level library should be used for the programming of the topic map. The library d3.js (data-driven documents)[1] was selected to produce the SVG image and determine its content with the help of Javascript code. Out of d3.js, the implementation of a force directed graph by Mike Bostock was used as anorientation for the implementation[2]. Using this graph implementation enables automatic placement of all nodes to ensure both, a good layout and visibility (see appendix A.2).

The main objects within the topic map are links and nodes. The nodes are associated with the key-terms placed within a graph. The links are the connections between those nodes.

Listing 3.16: Sourcecode that draws the SVG nodes.

```
1  <g class="node" transform="translate(600,300)">
2       <circle r="8" class="start"></circle>
3  </g>
4  <g class="node" transform="translate(624.1722067063263,159.22138081721977)">
5       <circle r="8"></circle>
6  </g>
```

Listing 3.16 shows the SVG code that is used to draw the nodes. In listing 3.17, the source code for displaying the links between the nodes is indicated.

Listing 3.17: Sourcecode that draws the SVG links.

```
1  <line class="link" style="stroke-opacity: 0.5168857799621697; stroke-width:
      3.1013726523199 7px;" x1="600" y1="300" x2="624.1722067063263" y2="
      159.22138081721977"></line>
```

The user starts interacting with the topic map, when he has finished writing an annotation. At first, he has to hit the "Create Topic Map Entry Points in Annotation" button to highlight keywords enhanced with a semantic context. Those are the keywords that could be identified through the semantic extraction process.

The user then has the opportunity to access the topic map by clicking on any of those key terms (see figure 3.25). The one he clicked at will then be in the center of the map and its context will be shown in the topic map. The map consists of a set of nodes connected to each other via links.

Each of the keywords has four different functions attached to them; they can be accessed by clicking the orange arrow. Those are

---

[1]http://d3js.org/
[2]https://gist.github.com/mbostock/4062045

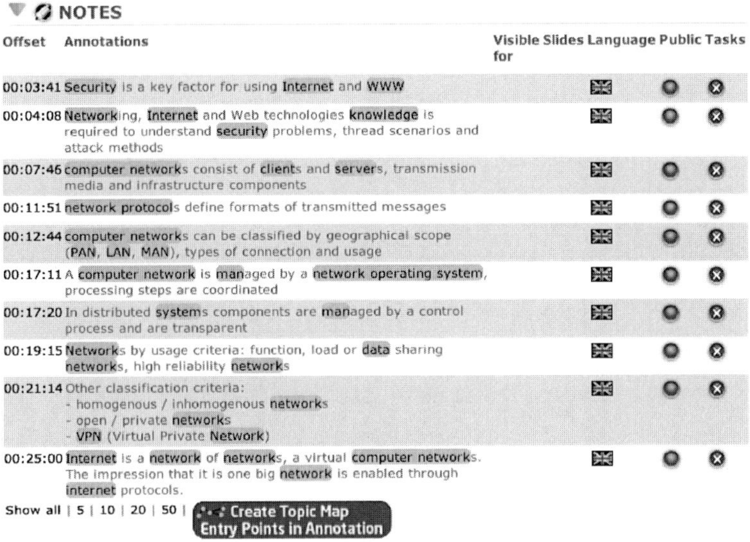

▼ **⚙ NOTES**

Offset	Annotations		Visible for	Slides	Language	Public	Tasks
00:03:41	Security is a key factor for using Internet and WWW		🏴	○	⊗		
00:04:08	Networking, Internet and Web technologies knowledge is required to understand security problems, thread scenarios and attack methods		🏴	○	⊗		
00:07:46	computer networks consist of clients and servers, transmission media and infrastructure components		🏴	○	⊗		
00:11:51	network protocols define formats of transmitted messages		🏴	○	⊗		
00:12:44	computer networks can be classified by geographical scope (PAN, LAN, MAN), types of connection and usage		🏴	○	⊗		
00:17:11	A computer network is managed by a network operating system, processing steps are coordinated		🏴	○	⊗		
00:17:20	In distributed systems components are managed by a control process and are transparent		🏴	○	⊗		
00:19:15	Networks by usage criteria: function, load or data sharing networks, high reliability networks		🏴	○	⊗		
00:21:14	Other classification criteria: - homogenous / inhomogenous networks - open / private networks - VPN (Virtual Private Network)		🏴	○	⊗		
00:25:00	Internet is a network of networks, a virtual computer networks. The impression that it is one big network is enabled through internet protocols.		🏴	○	⊗		

Show all | 5 | 10 | 20 | 50 | **⊙⊙ ∴ Create Topic Map Entry Points in Annotation**

Figure 3.25: Screenshot of the entry points to the semantic topic map in the annotation

- search for keyword in the global portal search,

- access the Wikipedia entry to the keyword,

- play best video to the entry and

- navigate to the keywords' own topic map to see its context.

These functions shall assist the user in finding related content items or further information about the topic once he got an overview of it. With those basic function, we can only help the user to find other videos within our portal and access basic information about the word through the encyclopaedia Wikipedia. The final source code in the browser drawing the node labels and the icons links with the additional functions is shown in listing A.3.

The semantic context of the key-terms allows to be extended by a variety of other functions. Books, research papers as well as related lectures from other lecture video portals might be recommended. But since the aim was testing the acceptance of the topic map in general, the focus was not put on the recommendation part.

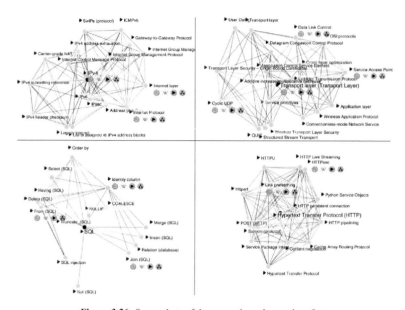

Figure 3.26: Screenshots of the semantic topic map interface

Because it should be visible in the graph which key term is connected to which other keyword and by which strength, the links between them have different width and transparency. The thicker and darker the line, the stronger the connection between the terms. Looking at the graph, it is obvious that with a growing amount of data in one graph, the labels will be overlapping. This is especially the case when the icons for further functionality are all visible. Two techniques were used to deal with this issue. First of all force-based label placement by Moritz Stefaner [1] was adopted to the prototype in this work to place the node labels as well as link icons within the graph. Second, the link icons have to be opened for each keyword individually so that the user would only clicks those which he is interested in and the image would thus not be overloaded. In case words are still overlapping, the user would have the option to move around parts of the graph (see figure 3.26 for a view of the topic map interface).

---

[1] https://gist.github.com/MoritzStefaner/1377729

3.4 Discussion

The implementation of the basic Web 2.0 functions was straight forward and did not implicate too many problems. But in order for those functions to work properly and also fulfil their purpose within search and filtering modules, enough students have to participate. But user engagement is an issue, because not many students participate. For the rating functionality, calculating the rates over several content layers, was introduced as one solution to work against the lack of metadata and participation. However, this principle also only works with a minimum amount of metadata existing. The same problem appears with the tag cloud. It only gives a good overview of the topics, when a sufficient amount of tags were generated by the users. An alternative method to get more data into the tag cloud could be to utilize user-generated as well as automatically harvested keywords, for example from the OCR and ASR data, together. In this way the tag cloud would be usable also with a lack of sufficient user-generated metadata. This would on the other hand be opposed to the idea of giving an overview of the user's tags and might thus even discourage students from adding their own tags when those are not even visible anymore in the bunch of system build data.

This is why a different tool was suggested to take advantage of automatically generated metadata on the one side and bridge the gap between user-generated and machine harvested data on the other side - the semantic topic map that is hooked to user-generated annotations. Bridging the gap between Social Web data gained from Web 2.0 tools and the Semantic Web has been approached in many research projects, like for example (Gru07a, GBSR09, Kna10). The path taken in this work goes one step beyond previous research by encouraging the creation of data by the users and thus promote the active engagement on the one hand and leveraging the resulting data to contextualize key terms semantically on the other hand.

The lecture video annotation functions themselves need a lot of thoughts about usability in order to be successful. The next chapter about evaluation will go deeper into this topic. Furthermore the performance is quite an issue with the collaborative annotation function, as could be seen with preliminary tests in a seminar setting. Continuous requests to the database are necessary to keep the interface up to date with annotations of team colleagues. This results in a large number of queries which may lead to performance issues, especially when a lot of users are working with the system in parallel. Scalability thus needs be addressed thoughtfully by selecting appropriate server hard- and software that may handle enough database requests at a time. When the annotation function is used more heavily, it will also need to be integrated better with the search function by visualizing on a timeline basis where the keyword occurs and how often it occurs, allowing a direct jump into the video at this specific point in time. This was already suggested with OCR and ASR data by Yang (Yan13).

Looking at different results in the semantic retrieval process revealed, that the DBpedia Spotlight extraction service does not always come up with desired results. More experiments with different input parameters will be necessary to improve the outcome. Because the aim of the extraction process was to find out whether standard semantic relation finding algorithms could produce results being good enough to work as data providers for topic maps that will give users an overview of the topic and help with browsing, the fine tuning of the DBpedia spotlight algorithm was not in the focus of this work. In the test setup, the semantic information retrieval process was dependent on availability and speed of the online interfaces of the DBpedia and DBpedia Spotlight. This led to performance issues and down times. An offline version of the DBpedia should be used to eliminate this problem. When the results of DBpedia Spotlight cannot be optimized and the availability still is an issue in future tests, an own algorithm for matching keywords to semantic entities should be used. For the evaluation, the matching of entities and keywords will thus be processed manually in order not to have an influence of DBpedia's behaviour on the results.

For the remainder of this work, a comparison of the two ranking algorithms will be tackled in order to be able to decide which of those is best in the context of tele-teaching. Because it is very subjective, which results really matter in each case, it is difficult to create a ground truth that those two algorithms can be tested against in terms of precision and recall. Another algorithm to compare with would also not yield the desired results, since especially the value for the users is relevant and not a benchmark that is not focused on the specific context of a student in tele-teaching. Therefore an expert review will be used to quantify the value of the two extraction algorithms.

The speed of the semantic extraction process needs to be worked on as well. Parallelization is one method which can save time. For example the neighbour retrieval algorithms can be processed simultaneously as can be the processing of the individual entities with the two neighbour ranking algorithms. In order to be able to provide a fluent user experience, either a lot of data needs to be pre-processed for the kind of application suggested in this work or the processing has to reach the real-time level. Since the basic data from the DBpedia is not updated very frequently, pre-processing and regular updates of some core keywords' semantic contexts (that could be collected from user tags, recent search terms or most prominent keywords in ASR and OCR data) in combination with real-time processing of key terms not extracted so far would be a way to go. Performance and availability questions were not addressed in detail in this work, because the focus was on the users and their needs.

In order to see how the implementations were accepted by the users and if the data - extracted with the help of standard semantic web methods - can fulfil the requirements for a learner's topic map, the next chapter will go into detail about the evaluations done for those tools.

Chapter 4

Evaluation

In this chapter the study of the manuscript and marker (in section 4.2) along with the evaluation of the semantic topic map (in section 4.3) will be elaborated on. An overview of all studies conducted can be seen in table 4.1.

This chapter begins with describing the research methods used for the evaluation and continues by explaining the different evaluations, starting with evaluations of the digital manuscript and marker functions followed by assessments of the semantic topic map.

4.1 Research Methods

In order to conduct the evaluations, a combination of research methods was used. One set of studies was executed with user tests in a laboratory situation. This is a good method to gather qualitative feedback and observation data at the same time. Both allow to look beyond assumptions one already had before and only liked to prove and may lead to new insights from the users. Because often what people say they would do or believe they think differs from what they really do and experience when the use a system (Nie01), user testing is essential when feedback about a system is required. Also when thinking about what they have done in an earlier time, users tend to say what they think the test leader might like to hear, what they think is appropriate to say and they rationalize and interpret their behaviour (Nie01). Therefore it is necessary to align the observation data with the verbal or written feedback of the users.

Users were invited to take part in a user test with pre-set tasks. The studies started with a recruiting questionnaire, in order to assure that all test participants had the same level of previous knowledge about the system and about the test lectures used. If any of the recruits had deviant knowledge, they were not invited to participate at the test. The test persons continued with a pre-test questionnaire collecting general information about the person, like age and sex as well as information about how often they use

NO	Research Object	Research Objective	Number of Subjects	Research Setting	Method qualitative	Method quantitative
1	e-Lecture annotation functions	Utilization of lecture video annotation functions in a MOOC setting	788 MOOC partici-pants	MOOC	-	Questionnaire
2	e-Lecture annotation functions	Motivation to use collaborative video annotation	558 MOOC partici-pants	MOOC	-	Questionnaire
3	e-Lecture annotation functions	Perception of manuscript and marker functions, learning effectiveness	12 students	Laboratory	Think Aloud Method, Question-naire	Questionnaire and Quizz
4	e-Lecture annotation functions	Comparison of analogue to digital manuscript writing, Comparison of individual to collaborative digital manuscript writing	14 students	Seminar	Questionnaire	Questionnaire
5	semantic topic map	user perception	7 students	Laboratory pre-study	Think Aloud Method and Interview	Questionnaire
6	semantic topic map	user perception	12 students	Laboratory main study	Think Aloud Method and Interview	Questionnaire
7	semantic context retrieval process	quality of the extracted data	5 experts	Expert study	-	Questionnaires
8	semantic topic map	user perception	558 MOOC partici-pants	MOOC	-	Questionnaire

Table 4.1: Overview of evaluations

certain technologies, tools or methods and to find out about their general attitude towards the tested items. This is necessary in order to be able to explain the differences if the results are not homogeneous. It was followed by the actual user test. Finally, a post-test questionnaire and an interview were undertaken. Both are used to capture the perception of the participants and gather insights on open questions as well as positive and negative aspects of the tools tested. In the respective sections 4.2.2 and 4.3.2 the precise data captured will be explicated. At the time the tests were developed no standardized questionnaire addressing all issues targeted in the studies was known. Combining several questionnaires would not have been feasible due to the length of the studies and because those were pilot tests. For those reasons the questionnaires used in the studies were developed newly for them.

A second set of studies utilized user tests in a field study setup. Field studies are used, when the artificial testing environment in a laboratory would influence the test too much and when the environment in which certain products are used is very important. The field study was again accompanied with pre- and post-test questionnaires for the before mentioned reasons. Two inspection sets were carried out with the help of online questionnaires. Those are a good method to gather a larger amount of quantitative data and reach a remote audience. Which exact data is collected for which purpose will be elaborated in the corresponding section 4.2.3.

A combination of different data was used in the evaluation. The user tests collected qualitative findings gained from the think-aloud method (NH06) and additional side-comments by the participants during the test and post-test interviews. Furthermore, the observation manager observed the attendees during the test. Since the sample size in most of the tests presented in this section is only as large as requested as minimum by usability researchers (ST03), (Nie94), (DR94) and thus does mostly not fulfill the requirements for a quantitative evaluation, the qualitative information is a relevant part of the evaluation result. It is therefore explained in detail, summarizing the most important findings gained from the users.

Quantitative output was gathered with the help of questionnaires on a 5-point Likert-scale (see (MG01), p. 274). In the larger scale questionnaire, statistical evaluation methods were applied as well. They will be explained in greater depth in the respective sections 4.2.1, 4.2.1 and 4.3.3.

4.2 Evaluation of the Digital Manuscript and Marker Functions

Some results of the evaluation of the digital manuscript and marker functions were previously published in (GYM13b), (YGBM13) and (Gru13).

A crucial factor for the success of the lecture video annotation functions is the user acceptance. In order to evaluate these functions several surveys and user tests were conducted. The aim was to gather the opinions, experiences and facts of the users while using the functions. To get a multi-angle view on the utility of the annotation functions, qualitative and quantitative, objective (a knowledge test) and at the same time subjective data (user feedback) was collected.

At first a large scale survey was conducted in order to quantifiy the interest in a lecture video annotation function as well as the influencing motivational factors. Therefore, a questionnaire was distributed in a MOOC (GMM⁺13a, GMTW13, GMM⁺13b). All students of one course were asked to judge the usefulness of video annotations in a personal setup and video annotations shared in a learning group.

In a user first test, the feedback of the participants was accumulated together with data measuring the learning effectiveness when using a lecture video in connection with the video annotation functions. The feedback and learning effectiveness measures were gathered in a laboratory test. The results were already published (Gru13, GYM13b, YGBM13). Leading the design of this study was the question: *May digital annotation tools in connection with lecture videos positively influence the learning effectiveness by helping students to keep more of the lecture content in mind?* A setup with the annotation functions was thereby compared with a video-only setup. In order to also have a comparison with other functions offered in conjunction with video lectures, the indexing features of the portal (YGM12) were the third setup for the comparison. The video indexing features included a table of contents, keywords and slide previews, all of which were extracted from the lecture video with the help of OCR and ASR algorithms.

For the purpose of comparing analogue note taking to writing notes with the digital annotation function, a second user test was lined up. The comparison with the digital annotation function was carried out in an individual as well as a group setup, each in a seminar setting. Again, the participants were asked to compare the different methods and their perception about different options.

4.2.1 Motivation of in-depth User Studies by Surveys in a MOOC

In order to motivate the realization of further in-depth user studies with the lecture video annotation function, this first section will introduce the results of a large-scale survey in a MOOC setting. The first paragraph aims at general feedback of the participants to this function whereas the second targets motivational factors to use a collaborative annotation mode.

Subjective Perception of the Usefulness of Video Annotation Functions in a MOOC Context

At the end of a six-week German MOOC (Massive Open Online Course) at openHPI (GMM⁺13a, GMTW13, GMM⁺13b) (see theory about MOOCs and openHPI in section 2.2.2) a questionnaire was sent out to the participants. Two questions about using digital video annotation in a remote learning scenario were asked. 42.3% of the 2726 active participants of the course completed the survey. The video annotation functions have not been implemented in the MOOC platform yet. Hence it was the aim of the survey questions to find out about the general perception of these functions without that the test persons actually used them so far.

The first question addressed the helpfulness of a personal video annotation function where users may add notes at any point in time within the video. From all the questionnaire participants (n = 1153) 68.3% (n = 788) replied to that question. The answers were positive with 29% (226/788) finding it very useful and 36% (285/788) rather useful (see fig. 4.1 on the left hand side). In summary 65% of all students answering this question had a positive attitude towards the learning video annotation. Only 9% (69/788) of the participants had a negative attitude right from the beginning. Considering the return rate of the questionnaire the positive bias has to be taken into account, though. But even when taking into account that eventually the other 31,7% of the MOOC participants do not see a sense in the function, a large amount of people is still interested.

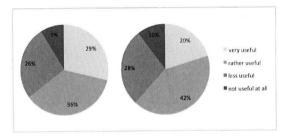

Figure 4.1: Perception of the personal annotation (left) and group annotation (right).

The second question aimed at evaluating the perceived utility of video annotations in groups where the note taker can write notes at any point within the lecture recording and share these notes among a learning group. 728 participants replied to this question. 20% (148/728) of them assessed the video annotation in groups as very useful and 42% (302/728) as rather useful (see fig. 4.1 on the right side). This adds up to 62% of the participants answering with a positive feedback about the video annotation in groups and only 9,6% (76/728) replying with a really negative answer.

This mostly positive feedback shows, that generally the attitude towards the utilization of digital video annotations, whether in an individual or group mode, is quite positive. But, as not all learners replied very positively, these results also reflect the theoretical position from the beginning of this thesis stating that lecture video annotations are appealing for learners with a specific learner style, but not for all learners (see section 2.2.3). Nevertheless, the digital video annotation in MOOCs is worth implementing. A second study was conducted in order to find out about motivation possibilities in terms of the culture of participation in a collaborative annotation scenario.

4. EVALUATION

Motivation Factors for Collaborative Annotation in a MOOC Context

In the second study in the context of the MOOC environment openHPI all currently registered users were invited to take part in the survey. These are about 62000 people. Nevertheless, the participants enrolled in the current course are only 9506, which explains the return rate of the questionnaire. Finally 558 users have answered the questionnaire.

With regard to the culture of participation design guidelines, the users were asked what would motivate them most to use a digital manuscript function. The wiki functionality and the newsfeed were the most popular functions with 36,2% (202/558) and 34,05% (190/558) replying with yes, totally or rather yes. A bit less than one third of the participants replied with no, not at all or rather no and about 25% had a neutral opinion.

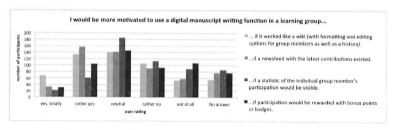

Figure 4.2: Motivation factors for collaborative video annotation.

Against the suggestions of the design guidelines of the culture of participation, the visibility of the performance of individual group members rather has a negative effect on the users' motivation to engage. 36,38% (203/558) answered rather no or no, not at all and 33,25% (185/558) hat a neutral opinion. Only 14,87% (83/558) replied with yes, totally or rather yes. This shows that publicly displaying the individual's performance is not a feature desired by the majority of the participants of this MOOC who answered the questionnaire. Nevertheless, the question whether those functions would actually have helped the learning process and especially the collaboration amongst the users, remains unanswered and should be considered for further research. When initially being demanded to use the culture of participation tools, the students might first see the benefits of them while using them.

Regarding the reward with badges the picture is not as bad, but surprisingly also not positive either. 24,19% (135/558) of the users replied with yes, totally or rather yes, 26,16% (146/558) neutral and 35,84% (200/558) with rather no or no, not at all. Those results show that also the opportunity for self-presentation within the group or gamification in order to show one's achievements only attracts a limited number of participants. One explanation for the diversity of the opinions and the reluctant attitude towards culture of participation principles could be the age distribution of the MOOC users. Nearly 30% are between 40 and 50 years old, 18% even between 50 and 60. 41% are between 20 and 40. Especially the older generation might be conservative towards current methods, like gamification. The conclusion is on the one hand that the publication of the individual's accomplishments, in every way (either via newsfeed, via rankings or via badges) should always be optional and users of the MOOC should not be obliged to use them. On the other hand ways to still introduce people to use those methods in order to overcome their reluctant attitude should be thought of.

Since the interest in the lecture video annotation functions could be shown quantitatively, user studies will be presented in the following paragraph that aimed at collecting insights and learning effectiveness data to those tools.

4.2.2 Evaluation of the Perception and the Learning Effectiveness of Lecture Video Annotation Tools in a Laboratory Setting

A testing environment in a laboratory setting with a previously prepared setup on a desktop PC was used to test the perception and learning effectiveness of lecture video annotation tools. Twelve male undergraduate or first semester graduate students in IT systems engineering were recruited for the test.

A website with a list of links to different videos that were used for each of the two tasks was prepared. The aim of the study was to compare the effectiveness and perception of different setups. Therefore a within-subject-design was used. But we needed to eliminate influences of learning and tiring effects. To counterbalance the conditions we randomly assigned each test person an order of the tasks and test videos for each task. Different videos had to be prepared for each of the conditions. We furthermore needed to avoid effects occurring due to differences in the previous knowledge of the participants. Therefore we started the recruiting with a questionnaire (see appendix B.1) levelling out this factor by pre-selecting participants. In our user study the first task concerned the evaluation of the indexing features in the tele-teaching portal (YGBM13). It will not be elaborated further, because it is not within the scope of this thesis.

Condition	Tools allowed
1	Video only
2	All Indexing Tools
3	Annotation Tools (Digital Manuscript, Marker)

Table 4.2: Listing of the conditions for the individual tasks in the laboratory study.

The second task asked participants to watch three different videos. Each video was about 10 minutes long. The participants were asked to memorize as much of the video content as possible. After each of the test conditions, a test paper (see appendix B.2) was given to the participants. While answering this paper the participants had no access to the lecture video or the notes they took while watching the video.

Different methods were used as measures and for data collection. The test leader wrote observations down. The time for completing the tasks was also taken. The learning effectiveness was tested with the help of test papers using multiple-answer and free text questions (see appendix B.3 for the results of the tasks). The answers were graded with points using three different methods, to ensure that the valuation method did not influence the result. In the first method (W1) +1 point was given for each correct and -2 points for each not selected or incorrect answer. +2 points were awarded for each correct result of the free text question. In the second method (W2) each correct answer was given +1 point, each incorrect -1 and 0 points were given for an answer not chosen. Free text questions were again granted +2 points per correct answer. The negative marking was used although it is not allowed in a German university context, because it is a method to increase reliability (LVS13), reward partial knowledge and penalize guessing (Bus01). The guessing might otherwise only be minimized by increasing the number of items in the test (LVS13), which could not be applied here since a video of 10 minutes length does not have material for more questions. Taking longer videos was not an option here either, since a within-subject-design was targeted. With longer videos the test would have been too long and tiring for the participants and thus influenced the results, since it already took about 90 minutes already including questionnaires and interview with the 10 minute videos. Because there was a maximum three correct answers, at the most six points were available for the free text questions. Three multiple-answer and one free text question had to be answered within one test paper. Since for each video the maximum number of correct answers differed, a third valuation method (W2 - normalized) was introduced. In order to equalize the maximum number of points of the different test videos, it included a weighted result of W2. Finally the question how do students perceived the video annotation tools had to be answered. A post-test-questionnaire (see appendix B.4) was used to test the different facets of each of the tools. Likert-scale items, free text questions along with tables listing pros and cons were included in the questionnaire.

In order to gather qualitative data, the participants were being observed while doing the tasks. Additionally a post-test-questionnaire was used to collect the subjective feedback about the tools. The following hypotheses were postulated according to our research question described in the first part of this section:

Hypothesis 4.2.2.1 *When using video annotation tools besides watching a lecture recording, users keep more content of a lecture video in mind.*

Hypothesis 4.2.2.2 *Users like video annotation tools and perceive them easy as well as fast and fun to use.*

In order to ensure a reliable comparison between the usage of the different tools tested and the video-only version, a within-subject-design was used. A within-subject-design uses one and the same test person to accomplish all given conditions as compared to the in-between-subject design which uses different candidates for all conditions. This allowed to ask the participants for a comparison of the different tools they were allowed to use. It thus has the disadvantage that there might be learning and tiring effect over time. The consequence is that the order of the conditions needs to be randomized. This results in more test persons needed in total, but still a smaller number of participants as would be required in a in-between-subject design. Because of the limited quantitative data that can be taken from the study and because the aim is to get a broader picture of the usefulness of the functionality, qualitative data plays a bigger role.

Quantitative Results

In order to measure the learning effectiveness of watching a lecture video with the help of different tools, we compared the results of the test paper in the three setups: watching lecture videos without additional tools, with the help of annotation functions and when using video indexing tools. When writing digital notes while watching a lecture recording, the learning effectiveness is higher (see fig. 4.3). A difference between the learning effectiveness when using video indexing functions or annotation features is also noticeable. The lowest score occurs when using the video-only version. Using indexing functions results in a higher learning effectiveness than learning with a video only version. The highest score in the paper was achieved in the condition with the annotation features. The results were not statistically significant. To ensure reliability a higher number of test persons would be needed.

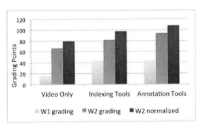

Figure 4.3: Evaluation of the learning effectiveness using annotation and indexing features.

Second, different questions were asked to gain the subjective perception of the tested functions by participation. Those questions were combined by a mean calculation in order to compute a common result of the perception and allow a quantification of the results. The question *"How do you evaluate the following tools?"* was divided into the following dimensions:

- The tool was easy to use.

- The tool was fast to use.

- The tool was fun to use.

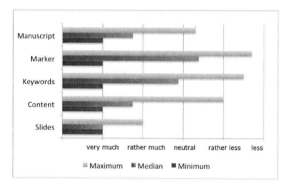

Figure 4.4: Evaluation of the overall perception of learning with lecture videos using annotation and indexing features.

A Friedman-test[1] was used in order to determine the significance of the tool perception ranking. Because the Friedman-test proved the statistical significance of the tool perception ranking, a Wilcoxon-test[2] was used in the next step to gather the significance values of the ranking steps. Because the evaluation only has an explorative character, no α-adjusting[3] has taken place.

In figure 4.4, the evaluation of the tool perception is visualized. Comparing the mean values, one can see that the slide preview is the most valued of the tools offered with a median rating of 1.0 (very good). The manuscript and contents features are

---

[1]The Friedman-test is statistical test that can be used for ranking repeated measures in order to for example find differences in the results when conducting several test attempts with different conditions(Fri37).

[2]The Wilcoxon-test is a statistical test used to compare differences between samples pairwise (Bor99).

[3]In statistics the likelihood that a alpha-error occurs rises the more is tested with one sample. α-adjusting, for example with the Bonferroni-correction, can be used to correct this error (VEHB10).

second with a median of 1.75 (good). The difference between the slide function and the two others is significant with p-values of 0.005 and 0.022. It is not possible to distinguish between the manuscript and contents function with statistical significance. The small sample size can only provide a tendency after all.

The keyword and marker functions received a rather neutral evaluation. In the next section about the qualitative results some reasons for that will be explained. The perception of the manuscript and marker functions differs significantly with a p-value of 0.002. With a p-value of 0.006 the perception of the manuscript and keyword functions is significantly different as well. The marker and keyword functions however are not evaluated differently.

Details of the questionnaire results also showed, that the marker function was not evaluated too positively in terms of speed, fun and easiness. In fact it was not used by many people at all. Reasons why will be explained in the following paragraph.

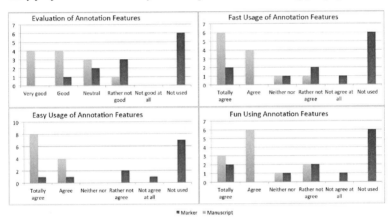

Figure 4.5: Evaluation of the perception of different annotation feature characteristics.

The manuscript function received much more positive feedback. Most of the participants agreed that the functionality is easy, fun and fast to use and gave it a good rating (see figure 4.5 for a graphical overview of this quantified observation, which can only be regarded as trend due to the sample size).

Qualitative Results

In this paragraph repeated user comments as well as the perception of the annotation function by the users will be illustrated. The observation and feedback revealed that usability is the key success factor for this function. One example is the marker function. It was necessary to scroll down the page to reach the marker input interface; therefore it was not often used by the test participants. This is also reflected in the questionnaire, where the feedback about the marker function was not too positive as well (see figure 4.5). Additionally, comments and observation revealed that students using the lecture recordings prefer having the video player including all the tools on one screen without the need to scroll (this was the case, because the video consumed most of the screen space). Feedback showed, though, that the functionality of the marker itself would have been useful to the participants for repeating parts of the lecture later on and revising for exams. The participants even offered some solutions to this problem themselves: Shortcut keys for a pre-set selection of markers or tagging of annotations with different marker types could be used instead of the existing marker function.

The test leader could observe that the test persons did not have any problems writing the digital notes while at the same time watching the lecture recordings. The participants positively commented on the speed and easiness of the functionality. They also said that because one writes condensed lecture content, the learning and revision process was positively influenced. The participants also liked the direct connection of the digital annotations with the video through a link on the timestamp. Some participants said that writing notes while watching lecture recordings had a positive effect on the concentration. Other test persons were not satisfied with the usability of the function and did not like the dual pressure when listening and writing parallel. They were also not totally happy with the time function of the manuscript feature. It only allows linking the annotation text to one specific point within the lecture by submitting the note once the note writing is finished (which usually is a point within the video when the topic dealt with in the note is already over). Finally, participants also asked for more editing and formatting options.

In summary one can say that both hypotheses have been confirmed for the manuscript function, but not for the marker feature. The benefits of using both features together showed a tendency for a positive influence on the learning effectiveness. The manuscript function was perceived as fun, easy and fast to use. The next chapter will describe a study researching the difference between manual and digital annotations as well as between digital group and personal annotations.

4.2.3 Evaluation of Individual and Group Annotations within the Scope of a Seminar

Within the setting of a seminar a second user study was conducted. 14 students, 3 female and 11 male, were asked to participate in the study while attending the seminar *Search Engine Optimization*. All of them took part in the study. Presentations had to be given by students in the seminar. Those were recorded with the lecture recording system tele-TASK. It was the goal of the study to find out which way of note taking during the lecture is preferred by the students in such a seminar setting. The varieties tested were analogue or digital notes and the two different digital versions individual and collaborative note taking in learning groups. In order to test the different conditions a within-subject design was used, meaning each student fulfilled tasks in each of the conditions. Two hypotheses were postulated for the test:

Hypothesis 4.2.3.1 *When watching a lecture or a presentation students prefer writing notes digitally more than to writing them manually.*

Hypothesis 4.2.3.2 *Users have a positive opinion about taking digital notes in a learning group.*

In an initial seminar session the students could try out all tools provided in the following sessions and familiarize themselves with the interface. In the following sessions they were then asked to write notes while watching the live presentations. All students wrote notes in the three conditions listed in table 4.3.

Condition	Tools used
analogue annotation	pen and paper
individual digital annotation	annotation interface in the portal
digital group annotation	annotation interface in the portal with the setting public to the group of seminar students

Table 4.3: Listing of conditions for the individual tasks in the seminar study.

After the participants had finished all conditions (which they all fulfilled in the same order, but within different appointments), a questionnaire was handed out. Several questions were given to them comparing the different conditions of note taking.

Quantitative Results

In order to quantitatively evaluate the users' perception of the digital annotation functionality, a combination of several questions within a questionnaire (see appendix B.5) was used. Because only 14 people participated in the test and not all of them answered the questionnaire completely, individual questions can only be evaluated on a qualitative basis. The answers to those questions together with the user feedback are elaborated next. A reliability test was used to check if all questions are sub-questions of the same overall question. Some questions were eliminated for the statistical evaluation afterwards. The Cronbach's α of the remaining six items is 0.79. Being larger than 0.7

101

this value implies that the reliability of the questions belonging together is sufficiently high (Kli99). The following statements were given to the test persons for rating on a Likert scale:

- I am satisfied with the digital note writing.

- I like the digital notes function.

- Writing notes with the tool has not distracted me from listening to the talk.

- I think it is helpful to use the time markers of the notes to retrieve a certain point in a video.

- Writing digital notes parallel to a live lecture is helpful.

- Writing digital notes while watching a recorded lecture is helpful.

The average evaluation of the digital manuscript function was a mean 2.78 (on a scale from 1 - best to 5 - worst), with a minimum of 2.0 and a maximum of 3.8. This evaluation is rather neutral and does not reflect well on the manuscript function. But looking at these numbers in more detail (see fig. 4.6) one can see, that a positive evaluation (from 1.0-2.5) was given by half of the participants (7/14) and a neutral one (2.6-3.5) by 6 people. Only one person evaluated the function negatively ($> 3, 5$).

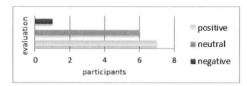

Figure 4.6: Evaluation of the manuscript function grouped by evaluation grade.

An interesting finding is that in general test participants who did not encounter problems when using the function gave a better evaluation (see fig. 4.7). Grouping the evaluation by participants' answer to the question "I had no problems using the manuscript function.", the persons saying they had no problems or answering that question neutrally evaluated the function positively (median 2.26/5) and the persons who had problems evaluating it rather neutral (median 3.2/5). The difference is not statistically significant.

In the following section the qualitative results, including a detailed description of individual questions of the questionnaire as well as an evaluation of the free text feedback from the participants and the observations will be described.

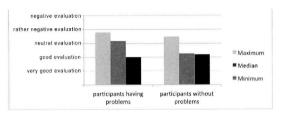

Figure 4.7: Evaluation of the manuscript function grouped by users having problems or not.

Qualitative Results

The participants were asked in the questionnaire how satisfied they were with the manuscript function and how they liked it. In order to be able to compare the subjective evaluation, the test persons were furthermore asked to evaluate how satisfied they were with the analogue note taking. The answers show that although most of the participants like the digital manuscript function, the analogue note taking satisfies them more (see fig. 4.8). Some of the reasons were described in the previous section. Quite a few students experienced problems they had not anticipated with the function. Some skepticism and not a lot of satisfaction are the results from these problems experienced. Improving the usability of the function will solve some of the issues and therefore most probably lead to higher appreciation.

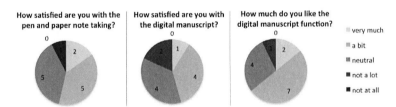

Figure 4.8: Satisfaction with manual compared to digital note taking.

Next, the students were asked to compare the manual and digital note taking according to the factors speed and fun. Combining those answers with the students' general attitude towards the two types of annotation, one can see that the students tend more towards the digital annotation. On average they found it more fun and faster and preferred the digital version (see fig. 4.9).

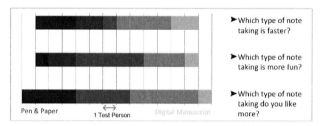

Figure 4.9: Comparison of perception, speed and fun of analogue note taking versus the digital manuscript.

Looking into the usage of the specific features the manuscript function offers, it was observable that a majority of the students (8/13) like the possibility to mark specific points within the video by making an annotation. They find it useful to be able to retrieve this information again later. Although most students (9/13) think it is a major advantage of the digital notes that those are searchable, they still want to be able to print them out and not only have them digitally (10/14 students agreed on that). In summary this means that the perfect note writing environment for students should combine the best features of the analogue and digital worlds.

It does not make any difference to the students when taking notes whether they create them while watching a recorded lecture or a live lecture. But, although the students see major benefits of the digital notes, they say they feel distracted from watching the lecture when writing notes at the same time. Interestingly the participants subjectively did not write more notes in the digital setup compared to the analogue variant. The expectation was differing due to the fact that computer science students key in data regularly and are very fast at it. The speed of writing being higher is mentioned by participants as an advantage, though. Half of the students experienced problems using the function. A bug that was eliminated after the first test for the following test rounds can explain this issue, as well as usability flaws in general.

The test participants had several wishes for further enhancements. A formular editor, like proposed in (Her11b), as well as shortcut keys for the marker function were desired features. Also the inclusion of images into the manuscript was asked for. Several students described that the timestamp of the annotation did not work for them. Because first they listen to the lecture, then they write the notes and when they finally submit the annotation, the point in the video where it belongs is over. Therefore a solution for placing the digital notes is required.

Manuscript writing in a learning group was the third test condition, because the manuscript function can be used in an individual and a group mode. A learning group for the whole seminar was created, where the seminar participants were asked to write and share annotations. Most of the participants (69% (9/13)) think writing digital notes in a learning group is meaningful. Only 16% (2/13) disagree or strongly disagree (see fig. 4.10).

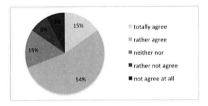

Figure 4.10: Evaluation of the collaborative manuscript writing function.

This positive attitude applies to a majority of the students (6/9), because they have a decent summary of the lecture afterwards and they can see what other learners do. Another benefit is that the students can save labor, because the note taking is shared among the students (3/9 students think so). It was interesting to observe that the students were shy to use the group function. Before they decided to become active themselves they first wanted to see what the other students did. For the test it would have been useful to have a longer trial and familiarization phase in order to avoid such effects, but this was not possible in the seminar setting.

In summary the hypotheses could be proven with a strong tendency. In order to substantiate the findings, more test persons would be needed. Because of the positive feedback it would be desirable to improve the usability of the user interface further, embed the annotation tool in a larger context of a didactical scenario and conduct another round of user tests.

4.3   Evaluation of the Semantic Topic Map

The study of the semantic topic map functionality is split into three parts. First, the quality of the semantic context that was retrieved utilizing keywords from the user-generated annotations is evaluated. The focus lies on finding out if the data generated with the automatic data extraction process is suitable for the exertion in a topic map. Second, the topic map interface is tested with users. To also gather some quantitative data about the function, a questionnaire is applied in a MOOC scenario.

4.3.1 Assessment of the Quality of the Semantic Context Retrieved from Web 2.0 Data

The quality of the semantic context retrieved from the web 2.0 data, specifically the user annotations to the lecture videos, was tested with the help of domain experts evaluating the data and the extraction process.

Because a large part of the semantic context retrieval algorithm is dependent on the third party implementations DBPedia and DBPedia Spotlight, data prepared beforehand was used for the evaluation. Specifically the creation of the annotations the user was going to write was prepared. The extraction of named entities from those annotations, that is carried out by the DBPedia Spotlight service in our automatic workflow, was done manually by the evaluators. This method was chosen, because the goal was not to evaluate those two external services, but to see if our retrieval process is sufficient for the task to retrieve a semantic context to user-generated texts. Also the availability of those third party services could not always be guaranteed during preliminary tests. Therefore the data was previously crawled and stored in our own database. Only the related entity finding and ranking processes were simulated for the evaluation in order to not be dependent on down-times of the DBPedia database.

Quality measures for this kind of algorithm can be precision and recall, which are basic metrics in information retrieval. We chose not to use those metrics for the evaluation, because a ground truth and algorithms to compare with would have been needed. The ground truth is difficult to create in this case, because it is very subjective, which kind of context is considered relevant for a certain key term. Also the goal was to find out if the data is suitable for the topic map context, which is a task that cannot be completed by comparison to another algorithm. Therefore an expert evaluation was chosen for the assessment of the retrieved context.

Five experts (PhD students and graduates in computer science) were asked to evaluate 30 topic maps for different keywords in order to ensure reliability of the evaluation across different data sets. The experts received the topic map in duplicate, if available, created with two different algorithms (algorithm 1 = log neighbour discovery, algorithm 2 = vector space model). They were then asked to rate the topic map in a questionnaire according to different criteria (see appendix B.6). The experts were first required to categorize the topic maps as narrow to broad topic on a 5-item Likert scale. Second they were invited to rate the selection of keywords within the topic map according to the following criteria:

- does it include wrong values (question 2)

- is it comprehensive enough (question 3)

- is the selection meaningful (question 4)

- does it give a good overview of the topic (question 5)

- does it give a good overview of related topics (question 6)

Generally 5-item Likert scales are ordinal data and thus need to be evaluated with different statistics methods than interval data. But in practice this type of Likert scales is mostly evaluated as interval data (Mog99, Jam04, Nor10). Therefore tests for the interval data level will be used.

In order to also ensure reliability across the experts, the inter-rater reliability is calculated. The inter-rater reliability is calculated using Cronbach's Alpha (LHC10). Cronbach's Alpha is a test that can be used for more than two raters, which makes it suitable for this scenario with five raters. It also takes the number of raters into account. Even with a low reliability across two raters the reliability rises the more raters have quite similar results.

	Rater 1	Rater 2	Rater 3	Rater 4	Rater 5
Rater 1	1,000	0,434	0,373	0,149	0,602
Rater 2	0,434	1,000	0,266	0,198	0,517
Rater 3	0,373	0,266	1,000	0,273	0,366
Rater 4	0,149	0,266	0,273	1,000	0,191
Rater 5	0,602	0,517	0,366	0,191	1,00

Table 4.4: Inter-rater reliability calculation with Cronbach's Alpha (α)

The results of these tests (see table 4.4) thus show that although reliability between each two raters is not sufficiently high (meaning at least > 0.7 for good results in Cronbach's Alpha), the overall weighted Cronbach's Alpha is 0.71, which is a good result. The result can even be improved when the results of rater four are not taken into account (see table 4.5). Cronbach's Alpha will then be 0.748. Therefore the results of rater four will not be considered for the evaluation.

	Rater 1	Rater 2	Rater 3	Rater 4	Rater 5
Cronbach's Alpha if Item Deleted	0,626	0,647	0,671	0,748	0,602

Table 4.5: Inter-rater reliability results without single raters.

Next, the individual algorithms shall be compared against each other. On the interval scale, the t-test can be used to accomplish this task (FH03, Bor99). Because the two algorithms might perform differently in the varied criteria, the disparity between the two algorithms is tested for each question individually.

For the t-test the results show a statistical significance between the two testing conditions when the result is <0.05. If the value is >0.05 one can conclude that the differences between the conditions are probably not due to the manipulation, but due

	Question 2	Question 3	Question 4	Question 5	Question 6
T-Test	0,171	0,002	0,627	0,724	0,724

Table 4.6: Statistical Comparison of the Algorithms with T-Test

to chance. The results in table 4.6 indicate that the algorithms only differ in question three (if the algorithm is comprehensive enough or not).

This quite similar behaviour of the two algorithms can also be deducted from the following diagrams. Those show the distribution of the Median values of the four raters. From the 30 keywords chosen for the evaluation, 30 topic maps could be generated for algorithm one (log neighbour discovery), but only 18 for algorithm two (vector space model). For the other 12 keywords algorithm two could not find any neighbours. Due to the difference in the number of available Median values, percentage is used as unit for the diagrams.

At first the experts were asked whether the topic map included wrong values (question 2) and second whether it was comprehensive enough (question 3). The results of both questions are visualized in figure 4.11. 83.3% (25/30) of the Median ratings for algorithm one determine that there are nearly no or no wrong values in the topic map. 77.2% (13/18) do so for algorithm two. 13.3% (4/30) say that there are some wrong values in the results of algorithm one and 22.2% (4/18) for algorithm two. Looking at these results in figure 4.11 on the left side one can summarize that both algorithms perform reasonably well in terms of the correctness of the results. Algorithm one performs a little bit better, but, as previously explained, this difference is not statistically significant.

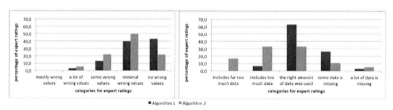

Figure 4.11: Evaluation of the correctness (left) and scope (right) of the semantic topic map.

Figure 4.11 on the right side visualizes the results of the question concerning the scope of the semantic topic map. The experts were asked whether the topic map contained the right amount of data, too much data or whether data was missing. 63,3% (10/30) of the Median of the expert ratings declared that the right amount of data was extracted by algorithm one and 33,3% (6/18) by algorithm two. Whereas for algorithm one 26,7% (8/39) topic map results were lacking some data, for algorithm two 50% (9/18) of the results included too much or far too much data. Those results can be linked to the results of the following three questions, which indicate that algorithm one is stronger in showing an overview of the exact topic whereas algorithm two is more likely to show related topics.

Figure 4.12 shows the results for the questions four (the selection makes sense), five (the selection gives a good overview of the topic) and six (the selection gives a good overview of related topics). The results are visualized for both algorithms using blue to green colors for algorithm one and yellow to orange for algorithm two. Generalizing the results one can say that both algorithms perform rather positive to neutral with differentiations in the single questions. 53,4% (16/30) Median ratings for the different topic maps show that the selection makes sense or rather makes sense for algorithm 1, 44,4% (8/18) of the results indicate that for algorithm two. 26,7% (8/30) for algorithm 1 and 33,3% (6/18) suggest neutral results in terms of the meaningfulness of the selection.

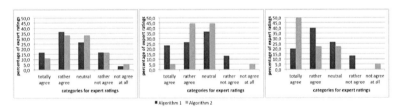

Figure 4.12: Assessment of the selection of relations within a topic map - it makes sense (left), it gives a good overview of the topic (middle) and it gives a good overview of related topics (right).

50% of the Median ratings suggest that algorithms 1 and 2 extract data that allows a good overview of the core topic of the topic map. 36.7% (11/30) are neutral for algorithm 1 and 44.4 (8/18) for algorithm 2. Those results look more promising when it comes to an overview of related topics. 60% (18/30) of all Median ratings for algorithm 1 and 72.2% (13/18) of those of algorithm 2 prompt a positive result in this criterion. This shows that both algorithms are in some cases able to show the overview of the specific topic, but are able to perform reasonably well in showing the context to a topic. The second algorithm operates even better in this criterion.

Because the expert evaluation results looked quite promising, the second group to be asked was potential users of the semantic topic map - the students. Those were IT systems engineering bachelor and master students unrelated to the author.

4.3.2 User Study of the Semantic Topic Map

Since the main research question for the semantic topic map is whether students are supported in gaining an overview of the topic and retrieving relevant information for learning with semantically enhanced topic maps, a user study with expert users of the sample tele-teaching portal tele-TASK was conducted.
The hypotheses for the usage of the semantic topic map are:

Hypothesis 4.3.2.1 *Users are supported in gaining an overview of the topic they want to learn with the help of the semantic topic map.*

Hypothesis 4.3.2.2 *Users can retrieve the relevant information for further learning within the topic from the topic map.*

Hypothesis 4.3.2.3 *Users find the connection of the semantic topic map to their personal lecture video annotation helpful.*

In this section, the results of a preliminary study with a high-fidelity prototype and the outcome of the final study will be elaborated.

Preliminary Study with a High-Fidelity Prototype

While implementing the semantic topic map that is connected with the digital lecture video annotation of the users, a high-fidelity prototype was built to gather preliminary test results for further usability improvements of the topic map. The prototype was created out of screen-mock-ups (see figure 4.13) that received a certain degree of hyperlinks and functionality via Microsoft PowerPoint functions. For the test persons it was possible to scroll down the page and see the annotations that were created for this test as if they were their own ones. By pressing the button "enhance my notes" some keywords in those annotations were highlighted. By clicking on these highlights, the semantic topic map for those keywords was opened up. In total three topic maps that were interlinked among each other were created manually for the purpose of this test. Some further functionality apart from the hypertexts links between the topic maps was available as well. The Wikipedia-icons led to the respective Wikipedia entry of the keyword and the play button opened the best suited video for that keyword.

Seven students of our institute were asked to participate in the study. They were shown the prototype, were given time to experiment with it and explore it by clicking through it. Afterwards they were asked what their first impression had been, how they would use the semantic topic map in a learning context, where they saw the advantages and disadvantages and which enhancements they suggested. Furthermore, the students were asked to answer three questions on a five-item Likert scale. The complete questionnaire is enclosed in appendix B.7.

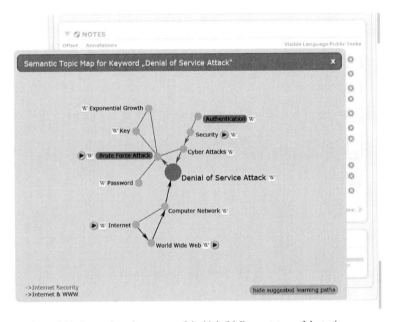

Figure 4.13: Screenshot of an extract of the high-fidelity prototype of the topic map.

The first impression of most of the students was overwhelming. They needed a moment to understand what it was and what it would be useful for. The students came up with different use cases in which they would apply this semantic topic map. Those manifold use cases are ordered in the list according to the number of of times they were mentioned starting with the most frequently stated one:

- Understanding the big picture: getting an overview of the topic area and its context as well as finding out which sub-topics belong to it.

- Finding a learning path: which prerequisites are there to learn a topic and work through a series of topics.

- Quickly navigating between videos with related topics.

- Using the map as starting point for further research, e.g. via the Wikipedia links.

Also the recommendations for further enhancements were very varied. The most common one was to change the name of the button to create topic map entry points, which we did for the final prototype. Other ones included usability issues, like showing connections between items more precisely, not showing unimportant items, limiting the number of items shown and offering hints at what to do with the map. Some enhancements were targeting further add-ons. One participant suggested having a tool tip for a preview of the video. Another one wished to add articles and books as well as a tool tip with further information about the item.

After the qualitative feedback we asked the participants three questions. Those questions were whether they consider the topic map useful, whether they find it intuitive to use and whether they think the combination of the semantic topic map with personal lecture video annotations is useful. An overview of the answers can be found in figure 4.14.

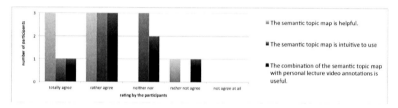

Figure 4.14: Evaluation results of the pre-study for the semantic topic map

The overview graphic shows that the topic map was rated very helpful or rather helpful by most of the participants and not helpful by only one participant. It also shows that there is potential for improvement when it comes to the intuitiveness of the usage of the topic map interface. None of the participants rated it negative, but three out of seven gave it a neutral rating. Therefore some considerations to usability were given before implementing the final prototype. The final question was posed concerning the combination of the semantic topic map with personal lecture video annotations. A majority of the participants found it very or rather useful, but one also not useful and two participants had a neutral opinion about it. Due to the small number of participants further investigation will be necessary on all of the questions, though. Nevertheless a more positive first evaluation result can be noted which leaves room for further adjustments.

Laboratory Study of the Topic Map with Cleaned Data

The final prototype was tested under laboratory conditions, in order to test the usability of the topic map function itself and not the underlying data. Again, a large part of the semantic context retrieval algorithm is dependent on the third party implementations DBPedia and DBPedia Spotlight. Therefore writing user annotations and extracting named entities from those annotations was done again manually by the evaluators. The related entity finding and ranking process was pre-processed as well.

12 IT systems engineering undergraduate and graduate students were asked to assess the topic map. The test participants were then asked to have a look at the annotations and try out the topic map functionality. They were asked to try out different maps, talk about their impression and think about potential uses of these maps. Thinking aloud was requested throughout this trial phase. The students were given a questionnaire at the end. They were questioned how they perceived the semantic topic map, whether they found the connection between the semantic topic map and the personal lecture video annotation function meaningful, what they thought about the advantages and disadvantages and which improvements they would suggest. Furthermore, they were asked to rate if they found adjacent topics, obtained a good overview of the topic, discovered related videos, if it was useful to navigate between keywords and navigate to the search function. The questionnaire used can be seen in appendix B.8.

Figure 4.15 shows an overview of the answers to the questionnaire questions. Because the number of test persons was small, the results of the pre-study are visualized additionally in order to have more data and thus be able to derive a tendency from the results. The chart is just used for visualization purposes, but should not be taken as quantitative evaluation due to the small sample size. The overview shows that the test persons tend to judge the topic map as rather positive.

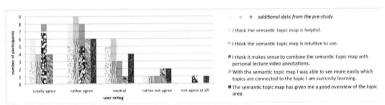

Figure 4.15: Evaluation results of the semantic topic map

The tendency is that the helpfulness and intuitiveness are rated as rather positive. The topic maps were evaluated a bit better at showing connected topics than at being able to give an overview of the topic area, but both were again judged rather positive. Most study participants agree that it is very useful to connect the semantic topic maps to the personal lecture video annotations.

The evaluation of certain functionality within the semantic topic map is not as clear as the general judgment just described. An overview of the ratings can be seen in figure 4.16). Whereas playing lecture videos directly from the topic map and navigating through topic maps between different keyword are assessed as being rather useful, searching for keywords of the topic map via the global portal search was judged quite diverse. Qualitative feedback revealed that some users regarded this function as obsolete when the instant-play of lecture videos is possible via the topic map.

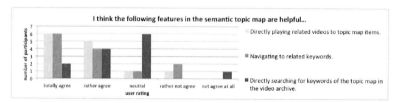

Figure 4.16: Evaluation results of features within the semantic topic map

Like in the pre-study the participants were questioned about their first impression. Several participants said right away that a visualization of topics was helpful and also found the keyword highlighting in the first step helpful. A majority of the test persons said that the first impression was overwhelming and confusing, because there is so much information and the animation was distracting them. When having had more time to explore the topic map, the students came to several use cases that are listed according to the number of times they were mentioned:

- Find out more details about the topic one is currently learning.

- Getting an overview of the topic and putting it in a context by finding out about relations between the topics.

- Expanding the search space by discovering connections to other topics.

- Have quick access to related information, like other videos or the Wikipedia page.

The use cases were quite tightly coupled with the advantages the test participants named:

- Quick, because visual, overview of topics and thus having more information on one screen.

- Good interface for browsing through topics and looking for interesting information by changing the focus within the maps.

- Improved likelihood of finding topics one would not have looked for otherwise (many students mentioned the same phenomenon when searching in Wikipedia. They start with one keyword and end up somewhere totally different after some time.)

- Connection to different media types. (Some students also suggested expanding the items offered by for example showing related literature or images).

The disadvantages can be deduced from the first impression. Sometimes the test participants found that the information was overlapping or that there were too many connections and it was therefore hard to track individual relations. Utilizing a 3rd dimension or highlighting the connecting lines of a knot with different colours when clicking on them where suggestions made. Otherwise usability issues like the adaption to screen sizes and a missing back-button were named. As further issues the participants stated that a certain number of user annotations is needed to create sufficient topic map entry points for browsing. This is no problem from the didactical perspective, since it should even improve the incentive to participate actively. Also the screen space the topic map needs makes it hard to use it while watching a lecture video. Since searching for new topics to look into while actively watching another video is not necessary, because the attention would have to be divided between the two different tasks and the performance in each task would thus decrease, which is counterproductive for both tasks (Wic91, p. 5).

The information that could be gathered during this laboratory study more likely describes trends in the usage of topic maps in connection with e-lectures and personal lecture annotations. Due to the small sample size no sufficient quantitative data could be collected. Therefore a questionnaire was sent out afterwards to a larger number of students within a MOOC to accumulate more data for quantitative predications.

4.3.3 Questionnaire in a MOOC setting

The participants of the openHPI MOOC were asked how helpful they consider an overview of the themes offered in the course and the connections between those topics in a topic map. Furthermore, they should rate how helpful they would find it to have topics in the topic map that are not addressed in the course. Also they were to estimate how often they would use it.

Figure 4.17 shows the evaluation results of the questionnaire. 38.17% (213/558) of the MOOC participants are not or less keen on working independently from the course layout. 26.7% (149/558) have a neutral opinion about it and only the remaining third is interested in leaving the beaten path. Since the survey was conducted in an xMOOC, which is rather oriented at traditional linear university learning, those results are not very surprising. If being conducted in a cMOOC scenario, the results would most

115

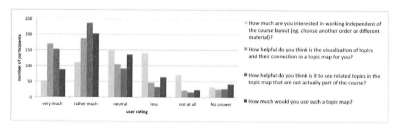

Figure 4.17: Evaluation results in a MOOC scenario concerning the users' interest in topic maps

probably have been different, because the cMOOCs are oriented more at connectivist style learning which implicates to leave beaten paths and search for individual own paths. This might also have an influence on the other results concerning the topic map, as users who do not want to find their own learning path do not need all the functionalities a topic map offers.

Nevertheless a majority of the participants (63.98% - 357/558) thinks that the visualization of topics and their connection in the form of a map would be helpful for them. Even more participants (69,71% - 389/558) would like to see relations to topics that are not specifically addressed in the course. A majority of the participants (52.15% - 291/558) additionally answered that they would use the topic map much or rather much.

This short quantitative study shows that there is quite a lot of potential for adoption of a topic map in a MOOC context. Although a majority of the participants is not interested in leaving the suggested learning path, they especially show interest in related topics and gaining an overview of the current topic. Specific use cases could be studies by splitting a sample group into people interested in learning off the prepared paths and students who prefer following a pre-build schedule.

4.4 Discussion

The studies described in this section support the hypotheses provided throughout this section. These stated that lecture video annotation functions and the semantic topic map can assist students in better learning with e-lectures. The first evaluation operated was the testing of the perception and learning effectiveness of working with the lecture video annotation functions. The marker function received rather neutral evaluation results. The observation showed that usability issues and especially the arrangement of the individual applications on the screen are major factors for the evaluation results.

The textual annotation tool manuscript received much more positive evaluation results. The test persons agreed that the function was fast, easy and fun to use. Especially this study could show a tendency that watching a lecture video while writing annotations enables students to perform better in a test afterwards. The results were the best using the annotation tool, second best using video indexing functions and worst with the video only version.

Those are very interesting findings since they suggest that writing digital annotations improves the learning effectiveness. This is one step beyond previous research, which proved that analogue note taking helps students learn (Kie89, BP05), because so far it was unclear if digital note writing is also beneficial for learning. Digital notes additionally offer for example the benefit of improved revision possibilities due to the linkage with the video, the option of collaboration and searchability. The result that digital annotations are preferred over analogue ones stands in contrast to findings of Steimle et al. (SBM09) who argued, that students prefer analogue note writing. But since this study was published (in 2009) the intuitiveness of the computer interfaces has improved a lot as has the ease of using these systems (BAMD13, FSG13). Therefore those findings may be deprecated. Especially when regarding the technical complexity of analogue note writing and digitization of those notes in post-production, the benefits of digital annotation become evident. Digital annotation is also easy to use, scalable as well as easily transferable back to an analogue derivative, if desired.

In a seminar setting manual annotations were compared to digital annotations. Furthermore, digital annotations in the individual mode were contrasted with those in a collaborative mode. Although again usability issues reduced the overall rating of the participants for the digital annotation function, they generally liked the digital version more than the offline option and also thought it was faster. Some of the features that only the digital variant offers were highly desired, but an analogue copy of the results was requested by the students as well. A majority of the test persons had a positive opinion about the collaborative manuscript writing. The results of a questionnaire returned by a large number of participants of a MOOC produced the same result. The second survey in a MOOC setting tackling questions about motivation factors for collaborative annotation revealed rather surprising insights, indeed. In contrast to the design guidelines for a culture of participation, the majority of the study participants replied not to be motivated by statistics of the individual group member's participation, bonus points or badges. This shows that the opportunity for self-presentation does not seem to be a desired function for everyone and should thus be optional.

One reason for this attitude can be the age distribution of the MOOC course, with more than half of the participants being older than 40 years. Due to this age distribution the likelihood that the users are less acquainted with digital technology in general and self-presentation and gamification specifically is higher. This lack of familiarity may lead to less confidence, which then results in less engagement (DGWT13). Another reason might be the self selection bias meaning that due to the low return rate the homogenity of the test group cannot be guaranteed. It might rather be the case that especially the people who strictly follow the pre-defined paths and given tasks were the ones also answering the questionnaire. Potentially those are also the ones who like a straight forward approach to learning without looking at their peers left and right from them. One way to also cater for those result- or exam-oriented students is by also scoring the student's action with collaborative tools and including those in the grading (Pop14). In contrast, features helping to work with the tool, like wiki formatting, a history and a newsfeed were found to be more motivating, which goes in line with the findings in (Her11a).

The semantic topic map was evaluated with different methods as well. A pre-study with users showed that the purpose of the topic map was to give an overview of the topic, assist in finding learning paths, be used for navigation in the lecture video portal and provide a basis for further learning and research. Participants rated the topic map as helpful and rather intuitive. The connection with the personal lecture video annotation was appreciated. Those findings were also supported in a laboratory test with the final prototype. Participants found the topic maps rather helpful for the use cases already stated for the pre-study. They also valued the connection with their personal annotations. Nevertheless some usability issues remain. In order to take full advantage of the visualization, a better highlighting and traceability of individual connections needs to be ensured, which is currently not the case due to the sometimes large number of items in the map. Also the quantitative evaluation in the MOOC context has shown that topic maps are highly desired and thus have a lot of potential to improve the learning experience.

The expert study revealed that both algorithms work reasonably well in extracting a semantic context to a keyword while at the same time only producing a minimal amount of wrong data. The algorithm using log neighbour discovery produces results for more topics than the algorithm using the vector space model. At the same time the amount of data generated is more suitable when using the log neighbour discovery algorithm. The log neighbour algorithm is better in retrieving related subjects whereas the vector space model algorithm performs slightly better in giving an overview of the topic itself. Thus one can conclude that both algorithms perform quite similar, with slight differences in some details. Therefore, joining the results of both algorithms to one final result is recommended. The results should be improved by for example filtering duplicates, researching about a proper maximum size of a category considered for neighbour entities and empirically determining a threshold for the similarity score of appropriate neighbours. The vector space model algorithm is presently only implemented for the structure of the DBpedia entity. As comparison and potential improvement to the two algorithms presented in this chapter, the vector space model algorithm for the content part of the DBpedia entity could be implemented.

In order to leverage the full potential of the functions described in this chapter, further improvements in the user interface design and usability of this interface need to be worked on. User tests are needed to confirm the success of the enhancements made. Especially with the semantic topic map different varieties of the map should be tried and tested against each other. One worthwhile extension would be to make the topic map customizable. The user should be able to decide on how many related subjects and how many steps from the main keyword the information should be visualized at the utmost. Furthermore, the kind of additional information displayed for the individual keyword should be customizable as well, because the preferences of the users were quite diverse.

However, some limitations exist for the studies. Looking at the results of the survey conducted in the MOOC setting one can see that the need of the users for such a structured overview is there. Specific use cases and in-depth user feedback can only be gathered with the help of a clickable prototype or the real application, though. For the user studies, first of all for some of the questions posed only qualitative data and little quantitative data could be gained. The reliability of the quantitative data gathered in the user tests could be improved by using a larger number of participants. Furthermore, the user studies were limited to IT systems engineering students. The surveys in the MOOC setting showed similar tendencies about the tool usage amongst a broader variety of people who are interested in internet technologies. Transferability to other disciplines and contexts can only be guaranteed through studies with representatives from those. Looking at these qualitative as well as quantitative results, main points for future work can be identified that will be elaborated in the next chapter.

4. EVALUATION

Chapter 5

Conclusion and Future Work

This thesis addresses the area of learning with e-lectures and explores technical ways to support learners in using lecture recordings within their knowledge acquisition process. The technical approaches focus on Web 2.0 and Semantic Web technologies, because they support collaboration and participation as well as information seeking. Those are two processes that are a major factors for learning effectiveness and the two main problems of tele-teaching this thesis aimed to tackle.

E-learning is an interdisciplinary topic which requires computer science competences for the implementation of tools and processes on the one hand, but also didactical knowledge for the content and the learning process support on the other. Psychology and social sciences are also involved in e-learning research, because e-learning deals with humans. With the interdisciplinary nature of e-learning in mind, this thesis was constructed using research methods from different disciplines in order to approach the problems from different perspectives.

5.1 Conclusion and Key Results

An overview of the current state of research and reflections on learning theory including the support of different learning styles led to the statement that current tele-teaching environments mostly aim at learners favouring the reflective observation mode and do not sufficiently support engagement and participation as well as contextualization of the content. In order to be able to contextualize content and supply search and filtering mechanisms, a sufficient metadata base also needs to be established.

As a consequence, the culture of participation design guidelines (Fis11) were identified as one possible solution to the collaboration and participation issue. Transferring those guidelines to the tele-teaching domain suggested, that different levels of engagement, awareness mechanisms and rewards for the user's contributions are missing in this e-learning branch. Collaborative digital video annotation was chosen as one example where to implement the culture of participation design guidelines, because previous research has shown that it overcomes problems of instructor-centric learning and fosters active learning (Pri04, Zup06, SYHZ10, REM11). Two annotation tools were developed and evaluated. The interpretation showed that the textual digital annotation function is helpful for learning as well as easy, fast and fun to use. As explained in the previous discussion, this moves one step beyond current research by showing a positive tendency for an improved learning effectiveness of digital annotation. The time marking tool was not used by the participants, due to usability issues. Hence, it became evident, that usability and extensive functionality of the tool is most important for its success. This is also supported by other research (RCM06, CHS$^+$05).

Major design guidelines for a culture of participation involving competitive elements were not desired in conjunction with the annotation tool in a MOOC context. This is surprising, because gamification, a new trend in e-learning, includes the same approach of fostering awareness for individuals' contributions and also creating a competitive aspect. One possible explanation is the age distribution of the MOOC the survey was undertaken in. In the user tests the qualitative feedback also showed that pure awareness is not attractive enough to motivate a more intense usage of the annotation functions. However, gamification was one solution offered by quite a number of test participants when being asked what could motivate them. Those contradicting results show that further investigation is necessary in order to improve the understanding of motivational factors for the tools described and to determine the role of gamification in this context. Previous studies mostly suggest that gamification yields positive results (HKS14). Nevertheless, future studies need methodological improvement, as also suggested by Hamari et al. (HKS14).

For the second aim of proving further opportunities for contextualizing the information and searching for content items, the automatic extraction of semantic metadata out of user-generated content was identified as an approach promising success. This path was chosen, because on the one hand tying the user's data to the context provides further benefit to the user. On the other hand only the connection to a semantic network actually allows to set the keywords in relation to other terms. This approach can be seen as parallel to the development of the World Wide Web, which moved from simple static content provisioning to participative Web 2.0 platforms and has begun to interconnect the individual services and content with the help of the Semantic Web in recent history. Previous research has primarily tackled the manual topic map building (MWC04, DD05c, Hie05, Pin10) in e-learning, which is very time consuming and thus does not fit to all learning scenarios. Since topic maps still have a lot of potential for contextualization, the combination user-generated content with automatic context retrieval was proposed in this work.

In order to address the user's need for contextualized information, semantic topic maps that are hooked to keywords in the user-generated annotations, were developed. The data for those maps was automatically retrieved from the large semantic knowledge base DBpedia. Several procedures to collect neighbours to a keyword in the knowledge graph were utilized. Two algorithms to rank those neighbours and thus determine the value of the relation were compared. An expert evaluation showed, that both algorithms perform reasonably well in delivering a context to a keyword, one explained the term itself in more detail whereas the other generated related topics. Therefore the approach of automatically generating topic maps via determining and ranking neighbours in a semantic graph is successful. Also the users agreed in user tests and surveys, that the topic maps are helpful and the connection between these and the users' annotations are meaningful. Those results could be confirmed in both, university and MOOC settings.

All in all, the evaluation results also support the findings deducted from learning theory (CJHL99, LR95), stating that different tools can support particular learner types. This has become especially apparent from the quantitative results of the questionnaires distributed in the MOOC. Whereas half of the participants had interest in the semantic topic map, only one third of them would use it more regularly. Also the annotation function would only be used regularly by a third of the learners. Nevertheless, the number of interested audience is large enough to implement the suggested tools in teleteaching environments, because they will enrich the learning experience for a certain type of learners. A variety of different functions and formats should be offered in any case in order to supply aid for each of the different learner types and thus reach a wider audience.

While this work was being finished, major advancements were made in the area of MOOCs. Several of the MOOC providers have also started implementing collaboration tools into their platforms. Nevertheless, although first experiments were started (BVL+13), thorough studies about which of those functions are really beneficial for students are still missing. Therefore, this work contributes a first step into the direction of evaluating and validating the usage and utility of certain tools in this specific learning context.

In summary, this thesis provides a number of contributions in the area of learning with e-lectures in university settings and in MOOCs:

- A survey of the theoretical background of the utilization of lecture recordings, including technical, pedagogical and human factors

- An overview of tools that may support different learning styles according to the model of Kolb when acquiring knowledge in a MOOC context

- The transfer of the culture of participation concept to the tele-teaching context which showed that theoretically awareness mechanisms and rewards for user's contributions need to be established. A basic evaluation of the culture of participation design guidelines with digital (collaborative) annotation functions in conjunction with e-lectures in a MOOC context showed, that a majority of the participants were not attracted to those offers in connection with personal lecture video annotations, though. Those opportunities for self presentation and gamification should thus always be optional.

- A confirmation that Web 2.0 tools cannot easily be transferred to the tele-teaching context and were thus not extensively used. Some possibilities to overcome this lack of user-generated data and still be able to make use of the value of those functions were proposed.

- An implementation and evaluation of digital lecture video annotation functions showing that those are helpful in both, university tele-teaching environments and MOOCs. Especially the comparison of the learning effectiveness using lecture video indexing tools versus the application of the annotation tool versus a video only version showed the tendency for an improved learning effectiveness.

- The development and testing of a semantic topic map suggesting that users consider the semantic topic map rather helpful as well as intuitive to use and favor the connection of personal lecture video annotations with semantic topic maps.

- A test implementation and evaluation of two algorithms to automatically extract a semantic context of user-generated annotations showing that the data gathered automatically is sufficient to present a semantic topic map. The evaluation included a novel approach which judged the algorithms with the help of expert's ratings. Whereas the log neighbour discovery algorithm rather gives an overview of the topic itself, the algorithm using the vector space model rather shows related topics. Which combination of the two algorithms is most helpful to the users remains to be researched.

Only the technical development is not enough, though. Embedding the tools in a didactical context is an important step as well, as already Ebner said when first discussing e-learning 2.0 (Ebn07) and Kerres and De Witt stated in their discourse about blended learning (KDW03). It is necessary in order to enable meaningful scenarios, fully leverage the potential of the tools implemented and create awareness amongst learners as well as teachers for the possibilities when using technology. In order to increase the appreciation of this potential and the understanding of the tools themselves, tutorials and trainings may be employed.

5.2 Future Work

In this work, the utilization of (collaborative) lecture video annotations as well as automatically generated topic maps were shown to be desired by the user and digital annotations also to improve the learning effectiveness. Nonetheless, a number of open issues and ideas for improvement remain, which will be highlighted in this section.

5.2.1 Lecture Video Annotations

In the field of lecture video annotations, several development opportunities exist. Additional features of the culture of participation should be implemented in order to gain a deeper understanding which of those functions works for which type of user in which learning scenario. A combination of tests gathering more information about the learner as well as utilization data in different scenarios is required to achieve this goal. A question in this context is whether improved awareness of the other people's contributions is enough to engage students in annotation activities or whether it would be even better to add gamification functions, like suggested by a number of research projects in the last year (DNDM⁺13, SRV13, HKS14). Considering that a majority of the students in a MOOC did not favour both of those options, a distinction between the contexts as well as the participants backgrounds and research about other motivational factors, like also suggested for e-learning in general by a number of researchers (All13, GRTG13, HMSU11), are necessary.

The usability of the functions developed in this work could be improved and the features integrated adapted further in order to fit the user's needs even more. In this context it would be interesting to compare the student's lecture video annotation process in a dedicated portal like it was shown in this work with the annotation process of tools they have already been using in other contexts, like twitter, facebook or a simple text editor. Twitter and Facebook were not chosen for this work, due to data security and privacy reasons (Rus11, YQH09), which are important criteria in e-learning in a university context (GHR09, MFDG12). Furthermore, a literature review by Manca and Ranieri showed, that there are many obstacles that prevent the adoption of Facebook for technology-enhanced learning (MR13). A pure text editor was not chosen either, because collaboration as well as hyperlinking video and annotation are not possible there. Nevertheless, especially large Web 2.0 platforms have a number of user friendly features and advantages. Comparing the different variants will allow insights into potentials of the other platforms that might be transferred to university internal video lecture portals in order to enhance them.

A next field currently researched is the exploitation of social connections for recommendation (BDBF⁺13, MKB10). This may also be used in conjunction with the digital video annotations and the semantic topic map in order to recommend certain lecture videos or parts within the video based on visits or annotations by friends or peers. To be able to do so a lot of user activity has to happen, though, which is why the participation issue is still a central one in this context.

Although digital annotations have been shown to be beneficial and desired by the students, the goals should still be to address the cognitive load of digital annotations (as already said in (SBM09)). Related studies showed that the cognitive load of using digital lecture supplemanting material (MRNCLB09) was higher than when using analogue material. Higher screen resolutions were found to reduce this obstacle though (MSK01). Since the technology has advanced a lot since those studies were undertaken and the students are more familiar with the devices, the cognitive load might be less now. This should be studied in more detail.

5.2.2 Topic Maps for E-Learning

The topic maps for learning have shown to have great potential in the sample tele-teaching scenarios used in this work. They have a lot of potential for further development in the tele-teaching context as well. More functionality can be integrated into those topic maps. For example it can be combined with a playlist or a backlog where a student can compile interesting topics and lectures for later study. The combination and integration of several Web 2.0 tools has also been identified as a good way to provide comprehensive support for e-learners in other recent publications (Pop14, SRT13). This finally leads to the ongoing discussion of Personal Learning Environments (PLEs). Whereas one group of researchers argues towards the one platform that allows the customizable integration of different learning tools and collection of learning content (CAJS10, SRT13), the other group rather advocates the free selection of individual tools and the consideration of the whole learning environment (not just the digital tool setting) as well as learning process from the whole human perspective (FV11, BAT11). The discussion remains undecided, but it still becomes clear that a sole focus on technical tools will not fulfil the requirements of providing a personal learning environment. Therefore again, the need of embedding tools in a certain learning scenario becomes evident.

Until now the best lecture matching was assigned manually to a keyword. This process can be automated in the future by improving the search function and using the highest ranked results as input source for the instant play function in the topic map. Alternatively a Vector Space Model approach can be considered a solution for the automatic matching as well. By building a vector of the entity's content and another vector of the lecture's content (which can be taken from either the OCR transcript or the ASR results), the lecture vector with the best similarity score with the entity vector can be an appropriate candidate for the best lecture-entity-match.

Since the topic maps are useful to get an overview of a topic and find related items one previously would not have thought of, they might be especially useful in informal, resource-based learning settings, where students are on their own when finding learning topics, learning paths and learning content. Resource-based learning has also been identified as one of the research challenges in e-learning (RB12). Initiatives like the

LinkedUp project[1] are currently working on integrating Open Educational Resources with the help of Linked Open Data to enable web-scale sharing and collecting of educational sources. A combination of this approach with topic maps could give a valuable visual overview of existing topics and resources to the user. The utility of topic maps in this context would be especially interesting to research, since graphical user-interfaces are being discussed as one possible approach to the problem of organizing resources (RB12). Combing resource-based learning with Semantic Web technologies has also been researched, for example in connection with semantic desktop systems for the personal information management (GHM⁺07).

An additional functionality within the topic map are learning paths. They were tested with the high-fidelity prototype but not yet implemented for the final result. A choice of learning paths is especially useful for self-directed or informal learning, where the students do not want to follow pre-defined lecture paths. In the case of a closed learning-environment, where lecture recordings are the basis, the learning path may be retrieved from the lecture order in the series by mapping the lecture titles to semantic entities. Another possibility is the utilization of ontologies. Within ontologies complex relations are modelled. With the help of query languages these can be queried. It would be interesting to investigate if it would be possible to extract reasonable learning paths from existing ontologies.

Finally, modifications of the visualization technique can be tried. First of all the existing topic map visualization can be parametrized in order to make it adaptable for the user and then tested again. The number of neighbours, thresholds within the neighbour distance and map size should be personalizable. During the user test, the inclusion of the 3rd dimension in the visualization was also suggested. This would be another visualization technique that the two-dimensional topic map could be compared with. Visualization techniques are used for the purpose of recommending and browsing.

Since the purpose of the topic maps is to give an overview of themes, help selecting content and support in creating own learning paths, more detailed studies should research if the topic maps are really more supportive in those tasks than text-only recommending and browsing interfaces, semantic search interfaces or tag clouds. Considering the content of the topic maps, the automatically harvested connections should be tested against manually created topic maps in order to quantify the qualitative difference between both.

5.2.3 Scaling up Learning and Learning Research

What e-learning research has quite often been lacking so far and where a lot of advancements can be made in the future is the number of test persons. New technology is often tested with a small sample size so that the number of quantitative results that

---

[1]http://linkedup-project.eu/

can be drawn from these studies is quite limited. Those studies are also mostly limited to a certain type of user, like the IT systems engineering university student in the case of this work.

With the scaling up of the learning, which addresses the advancement of the MOOCs on the one hand, new possibilities for research arise. Large numbers of users may contribute to the advancement of the underlying concepts and technologies. This opens up the opportunity to do large scale studies and quickly gain sufficient data for quantitative evaluations. Model based data analysis methods (KWG$^+$12) as well as the correlation of questionnaire data directly received from the user with log file data might provide new insights into learning processes. This way of evaluation will also be quicker than the previous qualitative studies where long tests with one person at a time were conducted. Being quicker, collecting massive data via questionnaires or log files will thus allow more iteration cycles. This will again lead to the possibility of comparing more varieties of tools and different versions of the tools.

Nevertheless, the quantitative data gathering and especially the lack of observation data, which often reveals insights the users would not have provided in a questionnaire (Nie01), also limits these studies. Because MOOCs are being undertaken in different subjects, this opens the opportunity of interdisciplinary testing scenarios. The important role of the differences between the academic cultures of the disciplines was stressed by a number of researchers (M$^+$08, TN05) and should thus also be considered in this context. Nevertheless, there is the additional difficulty of a broader variety of users with different backgrounds. This will lead to more influencing factors which might make it necessary to split the data in a number of groups and thus reduce the quantitative evidence and make assertions more difficult.

On the other hand, the previously mentioned Personal Learning Environments are another setting that can provide data from different academic disciplines and in general from a larger audience quantitatively. When the tools introduced in this work are integrated in a technical PLE environment, like for example (CAJS10, SRT13), they would be available for a whole university or institute giving access to all its students. Data could then be collected in lots of different use cases, but the test group itself would be more homogeneous than in a MOOC (different MOOCs show quite a broad diversity of participants (Wed13)), which makes it easier to draw assertions. Being present on campus, qualitative as well as quantitative data could be gathered with the university students in order to be compared.

The integration of different tools for learning and the combination of those tools with a social component are two of the main common ideas of MOOCs and PLEs. Whereas MOOCs focus on the massive aspect, PLEs rather aim at personalization and adaptability. Both approaches have their eligibility for different target groups. According to current criticism, MOOCs are not likely to overcome problems of university learning (Wed13, Mei13), whereas institutional PLEs especially target the learning of university students. Nevertheless, their ongoing popularity and numerous success stories of MOOCs have assured them a consideration in current research activities. Looking at the common ground of both approaches, adapting and researching the tools suggested in both scenarios will support the generalizability of the results gained in this work.

5. CONCLUSION AND FUTURE WORK

Bibliography

[AAF⁺96] ABOWD, Gregory D. ; ATKESON, Christopher G. ; FEINSTEIN, Ami ; HMELO, Cindy ; KOOPER, Rob ; LONG, Sue ; SAWHNEY, Nitin ; TANI, Mikiya: Teaching and learning as multimedia authoring: the classroom 2000 project. In: *Proceedings of the 4th ACM International Conference on Multimedia (MULTIMEDIA '96)*. New York, USA : ACM Press, 1996, S. 187 – 198 12

[All13] ALLEN, Michael W.: *Michael Allen's guide to e-learning: Building interactive, fun, and effective learning programs for any company.* John Wiley & Sons, 2013 125

[AMHWA⁺05] ALEMAN-MEZA, Boanerges ; HALASCHEK-WIENER, Christian ; ARPINAR, Ismailcem B. ; RAMAKRISHNAN, Cartic ; SHETH, Amit P.: Ranking Complex Relationships on the Semantic Web. In: *IEEE Internet Computing* 9 (2005), Nr. 3, S. 37–44 39

[AR03] ARMANI, Jacopo ; ROCCI, Andrea: Conceptual maps in e-learning: How map-based interfaces help the contextualization of information and the structuring of knowledge. In: *Information Design Journal* 11 (2003), Januar, Nr. 3, S. 171–184 22, 44

[AS13] ALLEN, I. E. ; SEAMAN, Jeff: Changing Course: Ten Years of Tracking Online Education in the United States / Babson Survey Research Group, College Board. Version: 2013. http://www.onlinelearningsurvey.com/reports/changingcourse.pdf. 2013. – Forschungsbericht 1

[AT05] ADOMAVICIUS, Gediminas ; TUZHILIN, Alexander: Towards the Next Generation of Recommender Systems: A Survey of the State-of-the-Art and Possible Extensions. In: *IEEE Transactions on Knowledge and Data Engineering* 17 (2005), Nr. 6, S. 734–749 40

BIBLIOGRAPHY

[Aus99] AUSSERHOFER, Andreas: Web based teaching and learning: a panacea? In: *Communications Magazine, IEEE* 37 (1999), Nr. 3, S. 92–96 10

[BÖ5] BÖNSCH, Manfred: Didaktische Landkarten und Lernpfade. In: *Fördermagazin* 5 (2005), S. 5–7 22

[Baa94] BAACKE, Dieter: Massenmedien. In: TIPPELT, Rudolf (Hrsg.): *Handbuch Erwachsenenbildung/Weiterbildung*. VS Verlag für Sozialwissenschaften, 1994, S. 455–462 19

[BAMD13] BETTINGER, Patrick ; ADLER, Frederic ; MAYRBERGER, Kerstin ; DÜRNBERGER, Hannah: Herausforderungen bei der Nutzung von Tablets im Studium Zur Relevanz der Gestalt der PLE , Lernverständnis und Entgrenzung. In: *GMW 2013*. Frankfurt, Germany, 2013, S. 62–73 32, 117

[BAT11] BUCHEM, Ilona ; ATTWELL, Graham ; TORRES, Ricardo: Understanding personal learning environments: Literature review and synthesis through the activity theory lens. In: *In: Proceedings of the The PLE Conference 2011*. Southampton, UK, 2011, S. 1–33 126

[Bat12] BATES, Tony: *What's right and what's wrong about Coursera-style MOOCs*. http://www.tonybates.ca/2012/08/05/whats-right-and-whats-wrong-about-coursera-style-moocs 2012. – [Online; accessed 20.10.2013] 19

[Bau10] BAUMGARTNER, Peter: Fachwissenschaft und Interdisziplinarität. Zur Begutachtung von fachübergreifenden Dissertationen am Beispiel von Arbeiten aus dem Themenbereich E-Learning. In: LENZ, W. (Hrsg.): *Interdisziplinarität - Wissenschaft im Wandel. Beiträge zur Entwicklung einer neuen Fakultät*. Wien : Löcker, 2010, S. 223–233 2

[BBGM09] BROOKS, Christopher ; BATEMAN, Scott ; GREER, Jim ; MCCALLA, Gord: Lessons Learned using Social and Semantic Web Technologies for E-Learning. In: DICHEVA, Darina (Hrsg.) ; MIZOGUCHI, Riichiro (Hrsg.) ; GREER, Jim (Hrsg.): *Semantic Web Technologies for e-Learning, Vol. 4*. IOS Press, 2009, Kapitel 14, S. 260–278 42

[BBMB07] BATEMAN, Scott ; BROOKS, Christopher ; MCCALLA, Gordon ; BRUSILOVSKY, Peter: Applying Collaborative Tagging to E-Learning. In: *Proceedings of the Workshop on Tagging and Meta-*

data for Social Information Organization (WWW'07). Banff, Canada : ACM, 2007 52, 55

[BCR11] BÖHNSTEDT, Doreen ; CHARD, Chris ; RENSING, Christoph: Interaktive Visualisierung von Wissensressourcen einer Lerncommunity und Modellierung eines Ressourcenpfads. In: *DeLFI 2011: Die 9. e-Learning Fachtagung Informatik*, 2011, S. 67–78 22

[BDBF⁺13] BERTINI, Marco ; DEL BIMBO, Alberto ; FERRACANI, Andrea ; GELLI, Francesco ; MADDALUNO, Daniele ; PEZZATINI, Daniele: A novel framework for collaborative video recommendation, interest discovery and friendship suggestion based on semantic profiling. In: *Proceedings of the 21st ACM international conference on Multimedia* ACM, 2013, S. 451–452 125

[BHBL09] BIZER, Christian ; HEATH, Tom ; BERNERS-LEE, Tim: Linked Data - The Story So Far. In: *Special Issue on Linked Data, International Journal on Semantic Web and Information Systems (IJSWIS)* 5 (2009), S. 1–22 37

[BKLI07] BIZER, Christian ; KOBILAROV, Georgi ; LEHMANN, Jens ; IVES, Zachary: DBpedia : A Nucleus for a Web of Open Data. In: *6th International Semantic Web Conference (ISWC 2007)*. Busan, Korea, 2007 36, 37, 70

[BKTS13] BÖRNER, Dirk ; KALZ, Marco ; TERNIER, Stefaan ; SPECHT, Marcus: Pervasive Interventions to Increase Pro-environmental Awareness, Consciousness, and Learning at the Workplace. In: *EC-TEL*, 2013, S. 57–70 66

[BLHL01] BERNERS-LEE, Tim ; HENDLER, James ; LASSILA, Ora: The Semantic Web. In: *Scientific American Magazine* 284 (2001), Nr. 5, S. 34–43 36

[BLK⁺09] BIZER, Christian ; LEHMANN, Jens ; KOBILAROV, Georgi ; AUER, Sören ; BECKER, Christian ; CYGANIAK, Richard ; HELLMANN, Sebastian: DBpedia - A crystallization point for the Web of Data. In: *Web Semantics: Science, Services and Agents on the World Wide Web* 7 (2009), September, Nr. 3, S. 154–165 38

[Blo56] BLOOM, B.S.: *Taxonomy of educational objectives: the classification of educational goals*. D. McKay, 1956 (Taxonomy of Educational Objectives: The Classification of Educational Goals v. 1) 55

[BLS99] BLISS, Joan ; LIGHT, Paul ; SHALJHO, Roger: *Learning Sites: Social and Technological Resources for Learning.* New York, NY, USA : Elsevier Science Inc., 1999 24

[Bod90] BODENDORF, F.: *Computer in der fachlichen und universitären Ausbildung.* Oldenbourg, 1990 (Handbuch der Informatik) 9, 10

[Bor99] BORTZ, Jürgen: *Statistik für Human- und Sozialwissenschaftler.* 5. Berlin, 1999 98, 107

[BP05] BOCH, Froncoise ; PIOLAT, Annie: Note taking and learning: A summary of research. In: *The WAC Journal* 16 (2005), Nr. September, S. 101–113+ 117

[Bre90] BRENDEL, H: Computer based training. In: *Der PC in Ausbildung und Schulung (IWT, 1990)* (1990) 9

[Bru66] BRUNER, Jerome S.: *Toward a Theory of Instruction.* Cambridge, MA : Belknap Press of Harvard University Press, 1966 24

[Bus01] BUSH, Martin: A multiple choice test that rewards partial knowledge. In: *Journal of Further and Higher education* 25 (2001), Nr. 2, S. 157–163 96

[BVL+13] BLOM, Jan ; VERMA, Himanshu ; LI, Nan ; SKEVI, Afroditi ; DILLENBOURG, Pierre: MOOCs are More Social than You Believe / eLearning Papers. 2013. – Forschungsbericht 123

[CA13] COCHRANE, Thomas ; ANTONCZAK, Laurent: Mobile Social Media as a Catalyst For Creative Pedagogy. In: *EC-TEL 2013 - Eigth European Conference on Technology Enhanced Learning.* Paphos, Cyprus : Springer, 2013 28

[CAJS10] CHATTI, Mohamed A. ; AGUSTIAWAN, Mohammad R. ; JARKE, Matthias ; SPECHT, Marcus: Toward a personal learning environment framework. In: *International Journal of Virtual and Personal Learning Environments (IJVPLE)* 1 (2010), Nr. 4, S. 66–85 126, 128

[CC96] CHEN, Yen-Tsung Herng-Yow an C. Herng-Yow an Chia ; CHEN, Jen-Shin Gin-Yi an H. Gin-Yi an Hong: An RTP-based synchronized hypermedia live lecture system for distance education. In: *Proceedings of the 7th ACM International Conference on Multimedia (MULTIMEDIA '99).* New York, USA : ACM Press, 1996, S. 91 – 99 13

[CHS+05] CHIU, Chao-Min ; HSU, Meng-Hsiang ; SUN, Szu-Yuan ; LIN, Tung-Ching ; SUN, Pei-Chen: Usability, quality, value and e-learning continuance decisions. In: *Computers & Education* 45 (2005), Nr. 4, S. 399–416 122

[CJHL99] CARVER JR, Curtis A. ; HOWARD, Richard A. ; LANE, William D.: Enhancing student learning through hypermedia courseware and incorporation of student learning styles. In: *IEEE Transactions on Education* 42 (1999), Nr. 1, S. 33–38 123

[CKR+07] CHA, Meeyoung ; KWAK, Haewoon ; RODRIGUEZ, Pablo ; AHN, Yong-Yeol ; MOON, Sue: I tube, you tube, everybody tubes: analyzing the world's largest user generated content video system. In: *Proceedings of the 7th ACM SIGCOMM conference on Internet measurement*. New York, NY, USA : ACM, 2007 (IMC '07), S. 1–14 18

[CM14] CHRISTOPH MEINEL, Jan Renz-Thomas S. Christian Willems W. Christian Willems: Reflections on Enrollment Numbers and Success Rates at the openHPI MOOC Platform. In: *Proceedings of the Second MOOC European Stakeholders Summit (EMOOCs2014)*. Lausanne, Switzerland, 2 2014 1

[Col96] COLLIS, BA: Tele-learning in a digital world: The future of distance learning. (1996) 9

[CRH+06] CHAN, Tak-wai ; ROSCHELLE, Jeremy ; HSI, Sherry ; KINSHUK ; SHARPLES, Mike ; BROWN, Tom ; PATTON, Charles ; CHERNIAVSKY, John ; PEA, Roy ; NORRIS, Cathie ; SOLOWAY, Elliot ; BALACHEFF, Nicolas ; SCARDAMALIA, Marlene ; DILLENBOURG, Pierre ; LOOI, Chee-Kit ; MILRAD, Marcelo ; HOPPE, Ulrich: One-to-One Technology-Enhance Learning: An Opportunity for Global Research and Collaboration. In: *Research and Practice in Technology Enhanced Learning* 1 (2006), Nr. 1, S. 3–29 9

[CW13] CHRISTIAN WILLEMS, Christoph M. Johannes Jasper J. Johannes Jasper: Introducing Hands-On Experience to a Massive Open Online Course on openHPI. In: *Proceedings of IEEE International Conference on Teaching, Assessment and Learning for Engineering (TALE 2013)*. Kuta, Bali, Indonesia : IEEE Press, 0 2013 23

[DD05a] DICHEV, Christo ; DICHEVA, Darina: Contexts as abstraction of grouping. In: *Proceedings of Workshop on Contexts and Ontologies,*

12th National Conference on Artificial Intelligence, AAAI 2005, 2005, S. 9–13 45

[DD05b] DICHEVA, Darina ; DICHEV, Christo: Authoring educational topic maps: can we make it easier? In: *Advanced Learning Technologies, 2005. ICALT 2005. Fifth IEEE International Conference on* IEEE, 2005, S. 216–218 45

[DD05c] DICHEVA, Darina ; DICHEV, Christo: Educational Topic Maps. In: *Fifth IEEE International Conference on Advanced Learning Technologies*, IEEE Computer Society, 2005, S. 950–951 22, 43, 44, 45, 122

[DDKN11] DETERDING, Sebastian ; DIXON, Dan ; KHALED, Rilla ; NACKE, Lennart: From game design elements to gamefulness: defining "gamification". In: *Proceedings of the 15th International Academic MindTrek Conference: Envisioning Future Media Environments*. New York, NY, USA : ACM, 2011 (MindTrek '11), S. 9–15 66

[DDL⁺06] DICHEVA, Darina ; DICHEV, Christo ; LUTHER, Martin ; JR, King ; SALEM, Winston: TM4L : Creating and Browsing Educational Topic Maps. In: *British Journal of Educational Technology - BRIT J EDUC TECHNOL* 37 (2006), Nr. 3, S. 391–404 45

[DDW05] DICHEVA, Darina ; DICHEV, Christo ; WANG, Dan: Visualizing Topic Maps for e-Learning. In: *Fifth IEEE International Conference on Advanced Learning Technologies ICALT05* Bd. 99, Ieee, 2005, S. 950–951 44, 45

[DGWT13] DE GEORGE-WALKER, Linda ; TYLER, Mark: Connected Older Adults: Conceptualizing Their Digital Participation. In: *The 4th International PLE Conference 2013 Berlin/Melbourne*. Melbourne, Australia, 2013 117

[DHK⁺11] DRUMMER, Jens ; HAMBACH, Sybille ; KIENLE, Andrea ; LUCKE, Ulrike ; MARTENS, Alke ; MÜLLER, Wolfgang ; RENSING, Christoph ; SCHROEDER, Ulrik ; SCHWILL, Andreas ; SPANNAGEL, Christian ; TRAHASCH, Stephan: Forschungsherausforderungen des E-Learning. In: *DeLFI 2011: Die 9. e-Learning Fachtagung Informatik*. Dresden : TUD press, 2011 1, 4, 16, 18

[DK07] DOGRU, Mustafa ; KALENDER, Suna: Applying the Subject "Cell" through Constructivist Approach during Science Lessons and the

Teacher's View. In: *International Journal of Environmental and Science Education* 2 (2007), Nr. 1, S. 3 – 13 24

[DNDM+13] DOMÍNGUEZ, Adrián ; NAVARRETE, Joseba Saenz-de ; DE-MARCOS, Luis ; FERNÁNDEZ-SANZ, Luis ; PAGÉS, Carmen ; MARTÍNEZ-HERRÁIZ, José-Javier: Gamifying learning experiences: Practical implications and outcomes. In: *Computers & Education* 63 (2013), S. 380–392 125

[DR94] DUMAS, Joseph S. ; REDISH, Janice C.: *A Practical Guide To Usability Testing*. Norwood, New Jersey : Ablex Publishing Corporation, 1994 91

[DZ11] DICK, Holger ; ZIETZ, Jason: Cultures of Participation als eine Persuasive Technologie. In: *i-com* (2011), Nr. 2, S. 9–15 26, 27

[Ebn07] EBNER, Martin: E-Learning 2.0= e-Learning 1.0+ Web 2.0? In: *Availability, Reliability and Security, 2007. ARES 2007. The Second International Conference on* IEEE, 2007, S. 1235–1239 124

[Ehl11] EHLERS, U.D.: *Qualität Im E-Learning Aus Lernersicht*. VS Verlag fur Sozialwissenschaften GmbH, 2011 (Medienbildung und Gesellschaft) 1, 9, 10

[EMC03] E.LEEUWIS ; M.FEDERICO ; CETTOLO, M.: Language modeling and transcription of the TED Corpus lectures. In: *Proc. of the IEEE ICASSP*, 2003 3

[EN93] ERTMER, Peggy A. ; NEWBY, Timothy J.: Behaviorism, Cognitivism, Constructivism: Comparing Critical Features from an Instructional Design Perspective. In: *Performance Improvement Quarterly* 6 (1993), Nr. 4, S. 50–72 24

[FENV09a] FOX, Patrick ; EMDEN, Johannes ; NEUBAUER, Nicolas ; VORNBERGER, Oliver: Integrating Lecture Recordings with Social Networks. In: BURDESCU, Dumitru D. (Hrsg.) ; CRESPI, Noël (Hrsg.) ; DINI, Oana (Hrsg.): *MMEDIA*, IEEE Computer Society, 2009, S. 18–22 31

[FENV09b] FOX, Patrick ; EMDEN, Johannes ; NEUBAUER, Nicolas ; VORNBERGER, Oliver: Vorlesungsaufzeichnungen im Kontext sozialer Netzwerke am Beispiel von Facebook. In: *Lernen im Digitalen Zeitalter - Workshopband*, 2009, S. 161–169 17, 31

BIBLIOGRAPHY

[FH03] FIELD, Andy ; HOLE, Graham J.: *How to Design and Report Experiments.* 1. Sage Publications Ltd, 2003 107

[Fis11] FISCHER, Gerhard: Understanding, Fostering, and Supporting Cultures of Participation. In: *interactions* 80 (2011), Nr. 3, S. 42 – 53 24, 25, 26, 27, 30, 121

[For10] FOREHAND, Mary: Bloom's taxonomy. In: *Emerging perspectives on learning, teaching, and technology* (2010) 23

[Fos96] *Constructivism. Theory, Perspectives, and Practice.* 1234 Amsterdam Avenue, New York, NY 10027 : Teachers College Press, 1996 24

[Fox11] FOX, Patrick: *Technische und soziale Konzepte von Vorlesungsaufzeichnungen in sozialen Netzwerken*, Universität Osnabrück, Dissertation, 2011 31

[Fri37] FRIEDMAN, Milton: The Use of Ranks to Avoid the Assumption of Normality Implicit in the Analysis of Variance. In: *Journal of the American Statistical Association* 32 (1937), S. 675–701 98

[FSG13] FISCHER, Nikolaus ; SMOLNIK, Stefan ; GALLETTA, Dennis: Examining the Potential for Tablet Use in a Higher Education Context. In: *Wirtschaftsinformatik*, 2013, S. 1 32, 117

[FV11] FIEDLER, Sebastian H. ; VÄLJATAGA, Terje: Personal learning environments: concept or technology? In: *International Journal of Virtual and Personal Learning Environments (IJVPLE)* 2 (2011), Nr. 4, S. 1–11 126

[FW08] F. WANG, T-C. P. C-W. Ngo N. C-W. Ngo: Structuring low-quality videotaped lectures for cross-reference browsing by video text analysis. In: *Journal of Pattern Recognition* 41 (2008), Nr. 10, S. 3257–3269 3

[GBBM09] GROSS, Andreas ; BAUMANN, Bert ; BROSS, Justus ; MEINEL, Christoph: Distribution to multiple platforms based on one video lecture archive. In: *Proceedings of the 37th annual ACM SIGUCCS fall conference.* New York, NY, USA : ACM, 2009 (SIGUCCS '09), S. 79–84 13

[GBSR09] GARCÍA, Renato D. ; BÖHNSTEDT, Doreen ; SCHOLL, Philipp ; RENSING, Christoph: Von Tags zu semantischen Netzen - Einsatz im Ressourcen-basierten Lernen. (2009), Nr. September, S. 29–36 87

[GCV+] GOVAERTS, Sten ; CAO, Yiwei ; VOZNIUK, Andrii ; HOLZER, Adrian ; ZUTIN, Danilo G. ; RUIZ, Elio San C. ; BOLLEN, Lars ; MANSKE, Sven ; FALTIN, Nils ; SALZMANN, Christophe ; TSOURL-IDAKI, Eleftheria ; GILLET, Denis: Towards an Online Lab Portal for Inquiry-based STEM Learning at School. In: WANG, Jhing-Fa (Hrsg.) ; LAU, Rynson W. H. (Hrsg.): *ICWL*, S. 244–253 23

[GH05] GOLDER, Scott A. ; HUBERMAN, Bernardo A.: The Structure of Collaborative Tagging Systems. In: *Journal of Information Science* 32(2) (2005), S. 198–208 52, 54

[GHM+07] GROZA, Tudor ; HANDSCHUH, Siegfried ; MOELLER, Knud ; GRIMNES, Gunnar ; SAUERMANN, Leo ; MINACK, Enrico ; MES-NAGE, Cedric ; JAZAYERI, Mehdi ; REIF, Gerald ; GUDJONSDOTTIR, Rosa: The NEPOMUK Project - On the way to the Social Semantic Desktop, JUCS, 2007, S. pp. 201–211 127

[GHR09] GRAF, Stephan ; HOMMEL, Wolfgang ; RATHMAYER, Sabine: Hochschulübergreifendes E-Learning: Technische Realisierung und Datenschutz. In: *Wirtschaftsinformatik (2)* Citeseer, 2009, S. 401–410 125

[GKK05] GOLDREI, S ; KAY, Judy ; KUMMERFELD, B: Exploiting user models to automate the harvesting of metadata for Learning Objects. In: *In Proc. of The Workshop on Adaptive Systems for Web-Based Education: Tools and Reusability*, 2005, S. 19–26 3

[GM07] GABRILOVICH, Evgeniy ; MARKOVITCH, Shaul: Computing Semantic Relatedness Using Wikipedia-based Explicit Semantic Analysis. (2007), S. 1606–1611 40, 78

[GM12] GRÜNEWALD, Franka ; MEINEL, Christoph: Implementing a Culture of Participation as Means for Collaboration in Tele-Teaching Using the Example of Cooperative Video Annotation. In: *DeLFI 2012 - Die 10. e-Learning Fachtagung Informatik*. Hagen, Germany : Gesellschaft für Informatik, 2012 16, 24, 25, 27, 28, 29, 57

[GM13] GRÜNEWALD, Franka ; MEINEL, Christoph: Social Semantic Keywords - Finding a Way to Enhance User-generated Metadata in Tele-Teaching - Poster Paper. In: *Gracehopper Celebration of Women in Computing*. Minneapolis, USA, 2013 34, 35

[GMM+13a] GRÜNEWALD, Franka ; MAZANDARANI, Elnaz ; MEINEL, Christoph ; TEUSNER, Ralf ; TOTSCHNIG, Michael ; WILLEMS, Christian:

openHPI - a Case-Study on the Emergence of two Learning Communities. In: *EDUCON 2013 - IEEE Global Engineering Education Conference*, 2013 1, 3, 4, 19, 92

[GMM⁺13b] GRÜNEWALD, Franka ; MAZANDARANI, Elnaz ; MEINEL, Christoph ; TEUSNER, Ralf ; TOTSCHNIG, Michael ; WILLEMS, Christian: openHPI: Soziales und Praktisches Lernen im Kontext eines MOOC. In: *DeLFI 2013 - Deutsche E-Learning Fachtagung der Gesellschaft für Informatik*, 2013 19, 22, 23, 92

[GMMS10] GROSS, Andreas ; MEINEL, Christoph ; MORITZ, Franka ; SIEBERT, Maria: Aufbau eines Multi-Plattform-Lernvideo-Archivs: Herausforderungen und Lösungen. In: HOHENSTEIN, Andreas (Hrsg.) ; WILBERS, Prof. Dr. K. (Hrsg.): *Handbuch E-Learning*. Wolters & Kluwer, 2010 50

[GMTW13] GRÜNEWALD, Franka ; MEINEL, Christoph ; TOTSCHNIG, Michael ; WILLEMS, Christian: Designing MOOCs for the Support of Multiple Learning Styles. In: *EC-TEL 2013 - Eigth European Conference on Technology Enhanced Learning*. Paphos, Cyprus : Springer, 2013 19, 20, 21, 22, 23, 26, 92

[Gre98] GREVEN, Jochen: *Das Funkkolleg: 1966-1998; ein Modell wissenschaftlicher Weiterbildung im Medienverbund; Erfahrungen-Auswertungen-Dokumentation*. Dt. Studien-Verlag, 1998 19

[GRTG13] GIESBERS, Bas ; RIENTIES, Bart ; TEMPELAAR, Dirk ; GIJSE-LAERS, Wim: Investigating the relations between motivation, tool use, participation, and performance in an e-learning course using web-videoconferencing. In: *Computers in Human Behavior* 29 (2013), Nr. 1, S. 285–292 125

[Gru07a] GRUBER, Thomas: Ontology of Folksonomy: A Mash-up of Apples and Oranges. In: *International Journal on Semantic Web & Information Systems* 3 (2007), Nr. 2, S. 1–11 36, 87

[Gru07b] GRUBER, Tom: Collective knowledge systems: Where the Social Web meets the Semantic Web. In: *World Wide Web Internet And Web Information Systems* 6 (2007), S. 4–13 36

[Gru13] GRUENEWALD, Franka: Implementation and Evaluation of Digital Video Annotation in Learning Groups to Foster Active Learning. In: *IEEE Transactions on Learning Technologies* (2013). – submitted for publication 57, 91, 92

[GS02] GRAND, Bénédicte L. ; SOTO, Michel ; GEROIMENKO, Vladimir (Hrsg.) ; CHEN, Chaomei (Hrsg.): *Visualizing the semantic web: XML-based internet and information visualization.* Springer, 2002. – 49–62 S. 43, 44, 45

[GS11] GROB, H. L. ; SCHNOOR, D.: Bessere Leistungen beim Lernen mit Multimedia - Ergebnisse eines Forschungsprojektes an der Universität Münster. In: *Learntec 97.* Karlsruhe, Germany : Karlsruher Kongreß- und Ausstellungs GmbH, 2011, S. 25–34 9

[GSJMB11] GARCÍA-SILVA, Andrés ; JAKOB, Max ; MENDES, Pablo N. ; BIZER, Christian: Multipedia: Enriching DBpedia with Multimedia Information. New York, New York, USA : ACM Press, Juni 2011, S. 137 40

[GSM11] GRUENEWALD, Franka ; SIEBERT, Maria ; MEINEL, Christoph: Leveraging Social Web Functionalities in Tele-Teaching Platforms. In: *International Journal for Digital Society* 2 (2011), Nr. 3 16, 27, 56

[GSSM12] GRÜNEWALD, Franka ; SIEBERT, Maria ; SCHULZE, Alexander ; MEINEL, Christoph: Automatic Categorization of Lecture Videos: Using Statistical Log File Analysis To Enhance Tele-Teaching Meta-data. In: *DeLFI 2012 - Die 10. e-Learning Fachtagung Informatik.* Hagen, Germany : Gesellschaft für Informatik, 2012 41

[GYM+13a] GRÜNEWALD, Franka ; YANG, Haojin ; MAZANDARANI, Elnaz ; BAUER, Matthias ; MEINEL, Christoph: Next Generation Tele-Teaching: Latest Recording Technology, User Engagement and Automatic Metadata Retrieval. In: *SouthCHI 2013 - International Conference on Human Factors in Computing & Informatics.* Maribor, Slovenia : Springer, 2013 11, 13, 16, 57

[GYM13b] GRÜNEWALD, Franka ; YANG, Haojin ; MEINEL, Christoph: Evaluating the Digital Manuscript Functionality - User Testing For Lecture Video Annotation Features. In: *ICWL 2013 - 12th International Conference on Web-based Learning.* Kenting, Taiwan, 2013 57, 91, 92

[Ham93] HAMMOND, Nick: Learning with hypertext: problems, principles and prospects. In: *Hypertext: A psychological perspective* (1993) 9

[Han97] HANNAFIN, Michael J.: Emerging technologies, ISD, and learning environments: Critical perspectives. In: *Educational Technology Research and Development* 40 (1997), S. 49–63 9

[HB08] HOSTETTER, Carol ; BUSCH, Monique: Student perceptions of collaborative learning, social presence and satisfaction in a blended learning environment: Relationships and critical factors. In: *Computers & Education* 51 (2008), Nr. 1 25

[Her11a] HERMANN, Christoph: Electures-Wiki - Toward Engaging Students to Actively Work with Lecture Recordings. In: *IEEE Transactions on Learning Technologies* 4 (2011), Nr. 4, S. 315–326 17, 31, 33, 118

[Her11b] HERMANN, Christoph: *Techniken und Konzepte für den Nachhaltigen Einsatz von Vorlesungsaufzeichnungen*, Albert-Ludwigs-Universität Freiburg, Dissertation, 2011 3, 11, 12, 13, 14, 104

[HHF09] HOFMANN, Cristian ; HOLLENDER, Nina ; FELLNER, Dieter: Workflow-Based Architecture for Collaborative Video Annotation. In: *Online Communities and Social Computing in Lecture Notes in Computer Science*. 5621. Heidelberg : Springer Berlin / Heidelberg, 2009, S. 33–42 30

[Hie05] HIERL, Sonja: Die Eignung des Einsatzes von Topic Maps für e-Learning. In: *Churer Schriften zur Informationswissenschaft* 4 (2005) 22, 44, 45, 122

[HK13] HAMARI, Juho ; KOIVISTO, Jonna: Social Motivations To Use Gamification: An Empirical Study Of Gamifying Exercise. In: *ECIS*, 2013, S. 105 66

[HKS14] HAMARI, Juho ; KOIVISTO, Jonna ; SARSA, Harri: Does Gamification Work?? A Literature Review of Empirical Studies on Gamification. In: *Proceedings of the 47th Hawaii International Conference on System Sciences. HICSS*, 2014 122, 125

[HL97] HANNAFIN, Michael J. ; LAND, Susan M.: The foundations and assumptions of technology-enhanced student-centered learning environments. In: *Instructional Science* 25 (1997), S. 167–202 9

[HMSU11] HERNANDEZ, Blanca ; MONTANER, Teresa ; SESE, F J. ; URQUIZU, Pilar: The role of social motivations in e-learning: How do they affect usage and success of ICT interactive tools? In: *Computers in Human Behavior* 27 (2011), Nr. 6, S. 2224–2232 125

[HS07] HAWK, Thomas F. ; SHAH, Amit J.: Using Learning Style Instruments to Enhance Student Learning. In: *Decision Sciences Journal of Innovative Education* 5 (2007), Nr. 1, S. 1–19 22

[Hür03] HÜRST, Wolfgang: Suche in aufgezeichneten Vorträgen und Vorlesungen. In: *DeLFI*, 2003, S. 27–36 3

[Jam04] JAMIESON, Susan: Likert scales: how to (ab) use them. In: *Medical
Education* 38 (2004), Nr. 12, S. 1217–1218 107

[KBM01] KOLB, D.A. ; BOYATZIS, R.E. ; MAINEMELIS, C. ; STERNBERG,
R.J., ZHANG, L.F. (Hrsg.): *Experiential Learning Theory: Previous
research and new directions*. London: Lawrence Erlbaum, 2001. –
227–247 S. 20

[KC07] KIMMERLE, Joachim ; CRESS, Ulrike: Group awareness and self-
presentation in computer-supported information exchange. In: *International Journal of Computer-Supported Collaborative Learning*
3 (2007), Oktober, Nr. 1, S. 85–97 25

[KD11] KUMAR, Sheo ; DUTTA, Kamlesh: Investigation on Security in LMS
Moodle. In: *International Journal of Information Technology and
Knowledge Management* 4 (2011), Nr. 1 31

[KDW03] KERRES, Michael ; DE WITT, Claudia: A didactical framework for
the design of blended learning arrangements. In: *Journal of Educational Media* 28 (2003), Nr. 2-3, S. 101–113 124

[Kee96] KEEGAN, D.: *Foundations of Distance Education*. Routledge, 1996
(Routledge education books) 19

[Kie89] KIEWRA, KennethA.: A review of note-taking: The encoding-storage
paradigm and beyond. In: *Educational Psychology Review* 1 (1989),
Nr. 2, S. 147–172 117

[Kir04] KIRCHHÖFER, Dieter: *Lernkultur Kompetenzentwicklung - Begrif-
fliche Grundlagen*. Berlin, 2004 15, 24

[Kli99] KLINE, Paul: *The handbook of psychological testing*. London: Routledge, 1999 102

[Kna10] KNAUTZ, Kathrin: Semantische Suche in Tag-Clouds. 13 (2010), Nr.
3 87

[Kol84] KOLB, D.A.: *Experiential Learning: Experience as the source of
learning and development*. New Jersey : Prentice Hall, 1984 20, 22

[KSH10] KETTERL, Markus ; SCHULTE, Olaf A. ; HOCHMAN, Adam: Open-cast Matterhorn: A community-driven Open Source Software project for producing, managing, and distributing academic video. In: *Interactive Technology and Smart Education* 7 (2010), Nr. 3, S. 168–180 3

[KW12] KEIL, Reinhard ; WESSNER, Martin: Interdisziplinarität als Herausforderung fuer die E-Learning-Forschung. In: *i-com* 11 (2012), Nr. 1, S. 3–6 1

[KWG+12] KNIJNENBURG, BartP. ; WILLEMSEN, MartijnC. ; GANTNER, Zeno ; SONCU, Hakan ; NEWELL, Chris: Explaining the user experience of recommender systems. In: *User Modeling and User-Adapted Interaction* 22 (2012), Nr. 4-5, S. 441–504 128

[Lan06] LANDOW, George P.: *Hypertext 3.0: Critical theory and new media in an era of globalization*. JHU Press, 2006 30

[LG00] LEETIERNAN, Scott ; GRUDIN, Jonathan: Fostering Engagement in Asynchronous Learning Through Collaborative Multimedia Annotation. (2000) 31, 32

[LHC10] LIAO, Shih C. ; HUNT, Elizabeth ; CHEN, Walter: Comparison between Inter-rater Reliability and Inter-rater Agreement in Performance Assessment. In: *Annals Academy of Medicine* 39 (2010), Nr. 8 107

[LM10] LUCKE, Ulrike ; MARTENS, Alke: Utilization of Semantic Networks for Education: On the Enhancement of Existing Learning Objects with Topic Maps in $< ML >$ [3]. In: FAEHNRICH, Klaus-Peter (Hrsg.) ; FRANCZYK, Bogdan (Hrsg.): *GI Jahrestagung (2)* Bd. 176, GI, 2010 (LNI), S. 91–96 42, 44, 45

[LR95] LIU, Min ; REED, W M.: The relationship between the learning strategies and learning styles in a hypermedia environment. In: *Computers in human behavior* 10 (1995), Nr. 4, S. 419–434 123

[LRQ12] LEAL, José P. ; RODRIGUES, Vânia ; QUEIRÓS, Ricardo: Computing Semantic Relatedness using DBPedia. In: SIMOES, Alberto (Hrsg.) ; QUEIROS, Ricardo (Hrsg.) ; CRUZ, Daniela da (Hrsg.): *1st Symposium on Languages, Applications and Technologies*. Dagstuhl, Germany : Schloss Dagstuhl - Leibniz-Zentrum fuer Informatik, 2012, S. 133–147 39, 40

[LS89] LILLIE, Hannum W. H. D. L. L. D. L. ; STUCK, G. B.: *Computers and Effective Instruction: Using Computers and Software in the Classroom*. White Plains, NY : Longman, 1989 9

[LS12] LUCKE, Ulrike ; SCHROEDER, Ulrik: Editorial - Forschungsherausforderungen des E-Learning. In: *i-com* 11 (2012), Nr. 1, S. 1–2 1, 2

[Lum12] LUMMA, Nico: *Netbooks sind auch nur eine Phase.* `http://blog.chip.de/business-blog/2012/05/11/` `netbooks-sind-auch-nur-eine-phase/`. Version: 2012 32

[LVS13] LESAGE, Ellen ; VALCKE, Martin ; SABBE, Elien: Scoring methods for multiple choice assessment in higher education–Is it still a matter of number right scoring or negative marking? In: *Studies in Educational Evaluation* 39 (2013), Nr. 3, S. 188–193 96

[LYC+07] LAI, C.-H. ; YANG, J.-C. ; CHEN, F.-C. ; HO, C.-W. ; CHAN, T.-W.: Affordances of mobile technologies for experiential learning: the interplay of technology and pedagogical practices. In: *Journal of Computer Assisted Learning* 23 (2007), Nr. 4, S. 326–337 22

[M+08] MAYRBERGER, Kerstin u. a.: Fachkulturen als Herausforderung für E-Learning 2.0. In: *Offener Bildungsraum Hochschule Freiheiten und Notwendigkeiten. Medien in der Wissenschaft, Bd* 48 (2008), S. 157–168 128

[Mar98] MARSHALL, Catherine C.: Toward an ecology of hypertext annotation. In: *Proceedings of the ninth ACM conference on Hypertext and hypermedia* ACM, 1998, S. 40–49 30

[Mas00] MASON, Robin: From distance education to online education. In: *The Internet and Higher Education* 3 (2000), Nr. 1-2 11

[Mei13] MEISENHELDER, Susan: MOOC Mania. In: *THOUGHT & ACTION* (2013), S. 7 128

[Men13] MENDES, Pablo N.: Semantic Exploration of Open Source Software Project Descriptions. In: *Workshop Intelligent Exploration of Semantic Data at Hypertext 2013*. Paris, France : ACM, 2013 40, 78

[MFDG12] MAY, Madeth ; FESSAKIS, Georgios ; DIMITRACOPOULOU, An-
gelique ; GEORGE, Sébastien: A Study on User's Perception in E-
learning Security and Privacy Issues. In: *Advanced Learning Technologies (ICALT), 2012 IEEE 12th International Conference on* IEEE,
2012, S. 88–89 125

[MG01] MCDANIEL, C.D. ; GATES, R.H.: *Marketing research essentials*.
South-Western College Pub., 2001 91

[Mic06] MICHAEL KERRES: Potenziale von Web 2.0 nutzen. In: HO-
HENSTEIN, Andreas (Hrsg.) ; WILBERS, Karl (Hrsg.): *Handbuch E-
Learning*. München : DWD-Verlag, 2006 16, 17

[Mil97] MILIUS, Scheer A. F.: Lehren und Lernen mit dem Internet: Das Pro-
jekt Lehre 2000 des Instituts für Wirtschaftsinformatik der Universität
des Saarlandes. In: *PAE - Arbeitshilfen für die Erwachsenenbildung*
3 (1997), S. 11–20 10

[MJGSB11] MENDES, Pablo N. ; JAKOB, Max ; GARCÍA-SILVA, Andrés ; BIZER,
Christian: DBpedia spotlight: Shedding Light on the Web of Documents. In: *Proceedings of the 7th International Conference on Semantic Systems - I-Semantics '11*. New York, USA : ACM Press,
September 2011, S. 1–8 38, 72, 73, 74

[MKB10] MERTENS, Robert ; KETTERL, Markus ; BRUSILOVSKY, Peter: Social Navigation in Web Lectures: A Study of virtPresenter. In: *Interactive Technology and Smart Education* 7 (2010), Nr. 3, S. 181–196
31, 125

[MKV04] MERTENS, Robert ; KRÜGER, Anja ; VORNBERGER, Oliver: Einsatz von Vorlesungsaufzeichnungen. In: HAMBORG, K.-C. (Hrsg.):
*Good Practice: netzbasiertes Lehren und Lernen an Universitäten ?
Erfahrungen mit verschiedenen Einsatzszenarien von e-Learning an
der Universität Osnabrück*. epos Media, 2004, S. 79 – 93 12

[ML07] MCLOUGHLIN, Catherine ; LEE, Mark J.: Social software and partic-
ipatory learning: Pedagogical choices with technology affordances in
the Web 2.0 era. In: *ICT: Providing choices for learners and learning.
Proceedings ascilite Singapore 2007*, 2007, S. 664–675 16

[Mog99] MOGEY, Nora: So You Want to Use a Likert Scale? In: *Learning
Technology Dissemination Initiative* (1999) 107

[MR13] MANCA, S. ; RANIERI, M.: Is it a tool suitable for learning? A critical review of the literature on Facebook as a technology-enhanced learning environment. In: *Journal of Computer Assisted Learning* 29 (2013), Nr. 6, S. 487–504 125

[MRNCLB09] MACEDO-ROUET, Mônica ; NEY, Muriel ; CHARLES, Sandrine ; LALLICH-BOIDIN, Geneviève: Students' Performance and Satisfaction with Web vs. Paper-based Practice Quizzes and Lecture Notes. In: *Comput. Educ.* 53 (2009), September, Nr. 2, S. 375–384 126

[MSK01] MAYES, D. K. ; SIMS, V. K. ; KOONCE, J. M.: Comprehension and workload differences for VDT and paper-based reading. In: *International Journal of Industrial Ergonomics* 28 (2001), S. 367?378 126

[MSM10a] MORITZ, Franka ; SIEBERT, Maria ; MEINEL, Christoph: Community Rating in the Tele-Lecturing Context. In: *IAENG International Conference on Internet Computing and Web Services (ICICWS'10)*. Hong Kong : IAENG, 2010 17, 27, 51

[MSM10b] MORITZ, Franka ; SIEBERT, Maria ; MEINEL, Christoph: Improving Community Rating in the Tele-Lecturing Context. In: *5th International Conference for Internet Technology and Secured Transactions*. London, UK : IEEE Press, 2010 17, 27, 51

[MSM11a] MORITZ, Franka ; SIEBERT, Maria ; MEINEL, Christoph: Community Tagging in Tele-Teaching Environments. In: *2nd International Conference on e-Education, e-Business, e-Management and E-Learning*. Mumbai, India, 2011 17, 27, 52, 53, 55

[MSM11b] MORITZ, Franka ; SIEBERT, Maria ; MEINEL, Christoph: Improving Search in Tele-Lecturing: Using Folksonomies as Trigger to Query Semantic Datasets to extract additional metadata. In: *Proceedings of the International Conference on Web Intelligence, Mining and Semantics - WIMS '11*. New York, New York, USA : ACM Press, Mai 2011 34, 35, 42, 70, 71

[MST11] MOORE, Joshua L. ; STEINKE, Florian ; TRESP, Volker: A Novel Metric for Information Retrieval in Semantic Networks. In: GARCIA-CASTRO, Raul (Hrsg.) ; FENSEL, Dieter (Hrsg.) ; ANTONIOU, Grigoris (Hrsg.): *ESWC Workshops* Bd. 7117, Springer, 2011 (Lecture Notes in Computer Science), S. 65–79 40, 78

[MT10] MICAN, Daniel ; TOMAI, Nicolae: Web 2.0 and Collaborative Tagging. In: *2010 Fifth International Conference on Internet and Web Applications and Services* (2010), Mai, S. 519–524 18

[MWC04] MAICHER, Lutz ; WITSCHEL, Hans F. ; CARRADORI, Andrea: Moving Topic Maps to Mainstream - Integration of Topic Map Generation in the Users -. (2004), S. 1–3 44, 122

[NH06] NØRGAARD, Mie ; HORNBÆK, Kasper: What do usability evaluators do in practice?: an explorative study of think-aloud testing. In: *Proceedings of the 6th conference on Designing Interactive systems* ACM, 2006, S. 209–218 91

[Nie94] NIELSEN, Jacob: Estimating the Number of Subjects Needed for a Thinking Aloud Test. In: *International Journal of Human-Computer Studies* 41 (1994), Nr. 3, S. 385–397 91

[Nie01] NIELSEN, Jakob: *First Rule of Usability? Don't Listen to Users, 2001.* http://www.nngroup.com/articles/first-rule-of-usability-dont-listen-to-users/, 2001. – [Online; accessed 08-April-2014] 89, 128

[NMO+] NOIA, Tommaso D. ; MIRIZZI, Roberto ; OSTUNI, Vito C. ; ROMITO, Davide ; ZANKER, Markus: Linked open data to support content-based recommender systems. In: PRESUTTI, Valentina (Hrsg.) ; PINTO, Helena S. (Hrsg.): *Proceedings of the 8th International Conference on Semantic Systems - I-SEMANTICS '12.* New York, USA : ACM, S. 1–8 39, 40, 75, 76, 77, 78

[Nol10] NOLL, Michael G.: *Understanding and Leveraging the Social Web for Information Retrieval*, Hasso-Plattner-Institut für Softwaresystemtechnik, PhD thesis, 2010. – 15 – 48 S. 52

[Nor10] NORMAN, Geoff: Likert scales, levels of measurement and the "laws of" statistics. In: *Advances in health sciences education : theory and practice* 15 (2010), Dezember, Nr. 5, S. 625–632 107

[NP13] NOCON, Witold ; POLAKÓW, Grzegorz: Methods Enabling Web-Based Learning of Control Algorithm Implementation Using Experimental Pilot-Plants. In: *ICWL*, 2013, S. 234–243 23

[OB95] OTTMANN, Thomas ; BACHER, Christian: Authoring on the Fly. In: *Journal of Universal Computer Science* 1 (1995), Nr. 10, S. 706 – 717 11, 12

[OL06] OLOFSSON, Anders D. ; LINDBERG, J. O.: "Whatever Happened to the Social Dimension?" Aspects of Learning in a Distance-based Teacher Training Programme. In: *Education and Information Technologies* 11 (2006), Januar, Nr. 1, S. 7–20 24

[O'N05] O'NEILL, M.E.: Automated Use of a Wiki for Collaborative Lecture Notes. In: *Proc. 36th SIGCSE Technical Symp. Computer Science Education, vol. 37, no. 1*, 2005, S. 267–271 31, 33

[PD13] PETER, Sandra ; DEIMANN, Markus: On the role of openness in education: A historical reconstruction. In: *Open Praxis* 5 (2013), Nr. 1, S. 7–14 19

[PH02] PARK, Jack ; HUNTING, Sam: *XML Topic Maps: Creating and Using Topic Maps for the Web.* Addison-Wesley, 2002 43

[Pin10] PINTO, Marcos S.: Using topic map to create an e-learning environment: the topic of OSI model map. In: *Journal of Computing Sciences in Colleges* 25 (2010), Mai, Nr. 5, S. 258–264 44, 45, 122

[Pop14] POPESCU, Elvira: Providing collaborative learning support with social media in an integrated environment. In: *World Wide Web* 17 (2014), Nr. 2, S. 199–212 118, 126

[PP99] PALLOFF, Rena M. ; PRATT, Keith: *Building Learning Communities in Cyberspace: Effective Strategies for the Online Classroom.* 1. Jossey-Bass, 1999 17

[Pri04] PRINCE, Michael: Does active learning work? A review of the research. In: *Journal of Engineering Education* 3 (2004), S. 223–231 30, 122

[PSGM] PEPPER, Steve ; STRATEGY, Chief ; GARSHOL, Lars M. ; MANAGER, Development: *Lessons on Applying Topic Maps.* http://www.ontopia.net/topicmaps/materials/ xmlconf.html 45

[RB12] RENSING, Christoph ; BÖHNSTEDT, Doreen: Informelles, Ressourcen-basiertes Lernen. In: *i-com* 11 (2012), Nr. 1, S. 15–18 126, 127

[RCM06] ROCA, Juan C. ; CHIU, Chao-Min ; MARTÍNEZ, Francisco J.: Understanding e-learning continuance intention: An extension of the Technology Acceptance Model. In: *International Journal of human-computer studies* 64 (2006), Nr. 8, S. 683–696 122

[Rei07] REILLY, Tim O.: What Is Web 2.0: Design Patterns and Business Models for the Next Generation of Software. In: *Communications & Strategies* No. 1 (2007), Nr. 65, S. 17–37 4, 16

[REM11] REINHARDT, Wolfgang ; ENGBRING, Dieter ; MAGENHEIM, Johannes: Video-Annotationen in der universitären Lehre. Anwendungsszenarien und koaktive Software. In: *i-com* 10 (2011), Nr. 1, S. 58 – 65 28, 29, 30, 31, 66, 122

[Ren13] RENSING, Christoph: MOOCs–Bedeutung von Massive Open Online Courses für die Hochschullehre. In: *PIK-Praxis der Informationsverarbeitung und Kommunikation* 36 (2013), Nr. 2, S. 141–145 19

[RHPL01] ROWE, Lawrence A. ; HARLEY, Diane ; PLETCHER, Peter ; LAWRENCE, Shannon: *BIBS: A Lecture Webcasting System.* http://repositories.cdlib.org/cshe/CSHE4-01, 2001 13

[RK11] RUST, Ina ; KRÜGER, Marc: Der Mehrwert von Vorlesungsaufzeichnungen als Ergänzungsangebot zur Präsenzlehre. In: KÖHLER, Thomas (Hrsg.) ; NEUMANN, Jörg (Hrsg.): *Wissensgemeinschaften: Digitale Medien- Öffnung und Offenheit in Forschung und Lehre.* Münster, Germany : Waxmann Verlag GmbH, 2011, S. 229–239 15

[Rod12] RODRIGUEZ, C O.: MOOCs and the AI-Stanford Like Courses: Two Successful and Distinct Course Formats for Massive Open Online Courses. In: *European Journal of Open, Distance and E-Learning* (2012) 1, 20

[Rod13] RODRIGUEZ, Osvaldo: The concept of openness behind c and x-MOOCs (Massive Open Online Courses). In: *Open Praxis* 5 (2013), Nr. 1 19

[RPLZS13] RIVERA-PELAYO, Verónica ; LACIĆ, Emanuel ; ZACHARIAS, Valentin ; STUDER, Rudi: LIM App: Reflecting on Audience Feedback for Improving Presentation Skills. In: *Scaling up Learning for Sustained Impact.* Springer Berlin Heidelberg, 2013, S. 514–519 66

[RT11] RIZZO, Giuseppe ; TRONCY, Raphael: NERD : a Framework for Evaluating Named Entity Recognition Tools in the Web of Data. In: *Workshop on Web Scale Knowledge Extraction (WEKEX'11).* Bonn, Germany, 2011, S. 1 – 16 38, 73

[Rus11] RUSHKOFF, Douglas: *You Are Not Facebooks Customer.* http://www.rushkoff.com/blog/2011/9/26/

`you-are-not-facebooks-customer.html`. Version: 2011 31, 125

[SBM09] STEIMLE, Jürgen ; BRDIEZKA, Oliver ; MÜHLHÄUSER, Max: Co-operative Paper-based Annotation of Lecture Slides. In: *Educational Technology & Society* 12 (2009), Nr. 4, S. 125–137 32, 117, 126

[Sch07] SCHULMEISTER, Rolf: *Grundlagen hypermedialer Lernsysteme: Theorie-Didaktik-Design*. Oldenbourg Verlag, 2007 1

[Sei13] SEIDEL, Niels: Peer Assessment und Peer Annotation mit Hilfe eines videobasierten CSCL-Scripts. In: *DeLFI 2013*, 2013 31, 32

[Sie05] SIEMENS, George: Connectivism: A Learning Theory for the Digital Age. In: *International Journal of Instructional Technology & Distance Learning* 2 (2005) 15, 17, 19, 24, 25

[Sie12] SIEMENS, George: *MOOCs are really a platform.* `http://www.elearnspace.org/blog/2012/07/25/moocs-are-really-a-platform/`, 2012. – [Online; accessed 04-March-2013] 1, 3, 19

[Sim13] SIMPSON, Ormond: *Supporting Students for Success in Online and Distance Education*. 3rd. New York : Routledge, 2013 1

[SJG02] STEEPLES, Christine ; JONES, Chris ; GOODYEAR, Peter: *Beyond e-learning: A future for networked learning*. Springer, 2002 10

[Ski54] SKINNER, Burrhus F.: The science of learning and the art of teaching. In: *American Psychologist* 11 (1954), S. 221–233 24

[SM83] SALTON, G. ; MCGILL, M.J.: *An Introduction to Modern Information Retrieval*. McGraw-Hill, 1983 40, 80

[SM02] SCHILLINGS, Volker ; MEINEL, Christoph: tele-TASK - Teleteaching Anywhere Solution Kit. In: *Proceedings of ACM SIGUCCS*. Providence, USA, 2002 3, 12, 14

[SMHM10] SIEBERT, Maria ; MORITZ, Franka ; HAMBACH, Frank ; MEINEL, Christoph: Enriching E-Learning Meta Data with User Generated Playlists. In: *5th International Conference for Internet Technology and Secured Transactions*. London, UK : IEEE Press, 2010 27, 55

[SMM10a] SIEBERT, Maria ; MORITZ, Franka ; MEINEL, Christoph: Distributed Recognition of Content Similarity in a Tele-Teaching Portal. In: *2nd International Conference on Information and Multimedia Technology (ICIMT 2010)*. Hong-Kong, 2010 53

[SMM10b] SIEBERT, Maria ; MORITZ, Franka ; MEINEL, Christoph: Establishing an Expandable Architecture for a tele-Teaching Platform. In: *Ninth IEEE/ACIS International Conference on Computer and Information Science*. Yamagata, Japan : IEEE Press, 2010 14

[SOĐ08] STAPIĆ, Zlatko ; OREHOVAČKI, Tihomir ; ĐANIĆ, Mario: Determination of optimal security settings for LMS Moodle. In: *MIPRO 2008-31st International Convention on Information and Communication Technology, Electronics and Microelectronics*, 2008 31

[Spa09] SPAETH, Daniela: *Uni goes Facebook: Warum und wie das Tool social virtPresenter kooperatives Lernen fördern kann*, Universität Augsburg, Bachelor Thesis, 2009 31

[SRT13] SIMOES, Tiago M. C. ; RODRIGUES, Joel J. P. C. ; TORRE, Isabel de l.: Personal Learning Environment Box (PLEBOX): A new approach to E-learning platforms. In: *Computer Applications in Engineering Education* 21 (2013), Nr. S1, S. E100–E109 126, 128

[SRV13] SIMÕES, Jorge ; REDONDO, Rebeca D. ; VILAS, Ana F.: A social gamification framework for a K-6 learning platform. In: *Computers in Human Behavior* 29 (2013), Nr. 2, S. 345–353 125

[SS08] SCHROEDER, Ulrik ; SPANNAGEL, Christian: Lernen mit Web-2.0-Anwendungen. In: *Navigationen. Zeitschrift für Medien- und Kulturwissenschaften* 8 (2008), Nr. 1, S. 59–59 16, 17

[SS13] STEINMETZ, Nadine ; SACK, Harald: Semantic Multimedia Information Retrieval Based on Contextual Descriptions. In: CIMIANO, Philipp (Hrsg.) ; CORCHO, Oscar (Hrsg.) ; PRESUTTI, Valentina (Hrsg.) ; HOLLINK, Laura (Hrsg.) ; RUDOLPH, Sebastian (Hrsg.): *Proceedings of 10th Extended Semantic Web Conference (ESWC 2013) - Semantics and Big Data*, Springer, 2013, S. 382–396 39

[ST03] SCHWEIBENZ, Werner ; THISSEN, Frank: *Qualität im Web : Benutzerfreundliche Webseiten durch Usability Evaluation*. Berlin Heidelberg New York : Springer-Verlag, 2003 91

[Sta05] STAEMMLER, Daniel: *Individuelle Differenzen beim Lernen mit interaktiven Hypermediasystemen*, Universität Hamburg, PhD Thesis, 2005 22

[sta13] *Anzahl der Tablet-Nutzer in Deutschland von 2010 bis 2012 und Prognose bis 2016 (in Millionen)*. http://de.statista. com/statistik/daten/studie/256712/umfrage/ anzahl-der-tablet-nutzer-in-deutschland/. Version: 2013 32

[SW08] SACK, Harald ; WAITELONIS, Jörg: Zeitbezogene kollaborative Annotation zur Verbesserung der inhaltsbasierten Videosuche. In: GAISER, Birgit (Hrsg.) ; HAMPEL, Thorsten (Hrsg.) ; PANKE, Stefanie (Hrsg.): *Good Tags and Bad Tags - Workshop Social Tagging in der Wissensorganisation*, Waxmann Verlag GmbH, 2008, S. 107–118 31, 33

[SWY75] SALTON, Gerard ; WONG, Anita ; YANG, Chung-Shu: A vector space model for automatic indexing. In: *Communications of the ACM* 18 (1975), Nr. 11, S. 613–620 40, 78

[SYHZ10] SU, Addison Y. ; YANG, Stephen J. ; HWANG, Wu-Yuin ; ZHANG, Jia: A Web 2.0-based collaborative annotation system for enhancing knowledge sharing in collaborative learning environments. In: *Computers & Education* 55 (2010), Nr. 2, S. 752–766 30, 122

[TJB+08] TORNIAI, Carlo ; JOVANOVIC, Jelena ; BATEMAN, Scott ; GASEVIC, Dragan ; HATALA, Marek: Leveraging Folksonomies for Ontology Evolution in E-learning Environments. In: *2008 IEEE International Conference on Semantic Computing*. Los Alamitos, CA, USA : IEEE Computer Society, August 2008, S. 206–213 42

[TLH09] TRAHASCH, Stephan ; LINCKELS, Serge ; HÜRST, Wolfgang: Vorlesungsaufzeichnungen - Anwendungen, Erfahrungen und Forschungsperspektiven. Beobachtungen vom GI-Workshop 'eLectures 2009'. In: *i-com* 8 (2009), S. 62–64 17

[TN05] TAVANGARIAN, Djamshid ; NOLTING, Kristin: *Auf zu neuen Ufern!: E-Learning heute und morgen*. Bd. 34. Waxmann Verlag, 2005. – 276 – 296 S. 128

[Ueb96] UEBELE, R: Der Weg zum virtuellen Klassenzimmer. In: *PAE-Arbeitshilfen für die Erwachsenenbildung* (1996), Nr. 32, S. 79–85 10

[VAG+11] VERNADAKIS, Nikolaos ; ANTONIOU, Panagiotis ; GIANNOUSI, Maria ; ZETOU, Eleni ; KIOUMOURTZOGLOU, Efthimis: Comparing hybrid learning with traditional approaches on learning the Microsoft Office Power Point 2003 program in tertiary education. In: *Computers & Education* 56 (2011), Januar, Nr. 1, S. 188–199 3

[VEHB10] VICTOR, Anja ; ELSAESSER, Amelie ; HOMMEL, Gerhard ; BLETTNER, Maria: Wie bewertet man die p-Wert-Flut? Hinweise zum Umgang mit dem multiplen Testen - Teil 10 der Serie zur Bewertung wissenschaftlicher Publikationen. In: *Deutsches Arzteblatt International* 107 (2010), Nr. 4, S. 50–56 98

[W3C11] W3C: *DBpedia Spotlight*. https://www.w3.org/2001/sw/wiki/DBpedia_Spotlight. Version: 2011 73

[Wed13] WEDEKIND, Joachim: MOOCs–eine Herausforderung für die Hochschulen? In: *Hochschuldidatik im Zeichen von Heterogenität und Vielfalt. Doppelfestschrift für Peter Baumgartner und Rolf Schulmeister.* (2013), S. 45–62 128

[Wen98] WENGER, Etienne: *Communities of Practice: Learning, Meaning and Identity*. Cambridge/MA : Cambridge University Press, 1998 24

[Whe12] WHEELER, Steve: *Recycling Kolb*. http://steve-wheeler.blogspot.de/2012/06/recycling-kolb.html, 2012 last viewed 18th of June 2013 23

[Wic91] WICKENS, Christopher D.: Processing resources and attention. In: *Multiple-task performance* (1991), S. 3–34 115

[Wil94] WILLIS, Barry D.: *Distance education: Strategies and tools*. Educational Technology, 1994 10

[WKE13] WILK, Stefan ; KOPF, Stephan ; EFFELSBERG, Wolfgang: Social Video: A Collaborative Video Annotation Environment to Support E-Learning. In: HERRINGTON, Jan (Hrsg.) ; COUROS, Alec (Hrsg.) ; IRVINE, Valerie (Hrsg.): *Proceedings of World Conference on Educational Multimedia, Hypermedia and Telecommunications 2013*. Victoria, Canada : AACE, June 2013, S. 1228–1237 31

[WKR+11] WILLEMS, Christian ; KLINGBEIL, Thomas ; RADVILAVICIUS, Lukas ; CENYS, Antanas ; MEINEL, Christoph: A Distributed Virtual Laboratory Architecture for Cybersecurity Training. In: *Proceedings of the 6th International Conference for Internet Technology and Secured Transactions (ICITST 2011).* Abu Dhabi, UAE : IEEE Press, 12 2011 23

[WLKS11] WAITELONIS, Jörg ; LUDWIG, Nadine ; KNUTH, Magnus ; SACK, Harald: Whoknows? evaluating linked data heuristics with a quiz that cleans up dbpedia. In: *Interactive Technology and Smart Education* 8 (2011), Nr. 4, S. 236–248 3

[WLM07] WOLF, Katrin ; LINCKELS, Serge ; MEINEL, Christoph: Teleteaching anywhere solution kit (Tele-TASK) goes mobile. In: *Proceedings of the 35th annual ACM SIGUCCS fall conference.* New York, NY, USA : ACM, 2007 (SIGUCCS '07), S. 366–371 13

[WM12] WILLEMS, Christian ; MEINEL, Christoph: Online Assessment for Hands-On Cybersecurity Training in a Virtual Lab. In: *Proceedings of the 3rd IEEE Global Engineering Education Conference (EDUCON 2012).* Marrakesh, Morocco : IEEE Press, 2012 23

[WSHK10] WAITELONIS, Jörg ; SACK, Harald ; HERCHER, Johannes ; KRAMER, Zalan: Semantically Enabled Exploratory Video Search. In: *Proc. of Semantic Search Workshop at the 19th Int. World Wide Web Conference.* Raleigh, NC, USA, 2010 43

[XML01] PEPPER, Steve (Hrsg.) ; MOORE, Graham (Hrsg.): *XML Topic Maps (XTM) 1.0.* http://www.topicmaps.org/xtm/, 2001 43

[Yan13] YANG, Haojin: *Automatic Video Indexing and Retrieval Using Video OCR Technology,* Hasso Plattner Institute, University of Potsdam, PhD thesis, 2013 3, 87

[YCS04] YANG, Stephen J. ; CHEN, Irene Ya-Ling ; SHAO, Norman W.: Ontology Enabled Annotation and Knowledge Management for Collaborative Learning in Virtual Learning Community. In: *Educational Technology & Society* 7 (2004), S. 70–81 30, 31, 42

[YGBM13] YANG, Haojin ; GRÜNEWALD, Franka ; BAUER, Matthias ; MEINEL, Christoph: Lecture Video Browsing Using Multimodal Information Resources. In: *ICWL 2013 - 12th International Conference on Web-based Learning.* Kenting, Taiwan, 2013 35, 91, 92, 95

[YGM12] YANG, Haojin ; GRÜNEWALD, Franka ; MEINEL, Christoph: Automated Extraction of Lecture Outlines From Lecture Videos - A Hybrid Solution for Lecture Video Indexing. In: *4th International Conference on Computer Supported Education.* Porto, Portugal, 2012, S. 13–22 4, 35, 92

[YL03]   YANG, Hsin-Chang ; LEE, Chung-Hong: Building Topic Maps Using a Text Mining Approach. In: ZHONG, Ning (Hrsg.) ; RAS, Zbigniew W. (Hrsg.) ; TSUMOTO, Shusaku (Hrsg.) ; SUZUKI, Einoshin (Hrsg.): *ISMIS* Bd. 2871, Springer, 2003 (Lecture Notes in Computer Science), S. 307–314 45

[YPDD12]   YU, Hong Q. ; PEDRINACI, Carlos ; DIETZE, Stefan ; DOMINGUE, John: Using Linked Data to Annotate and Search Educational Video Resources for Supporting Distance Learning. In: *IEEE Transactions on Learning Technologies* 5 (2012), April, Nr. 2, S. 130–142 31, 38, 42, 43

[YQH09]   YOUNG, Alyson L. ; QUAN-HAASE, Anabel: Information revelation and internet privacy concerns on social network sites: a case study of facebook. In: *Proceedings of the fourth international conference on Communities and technologies* ACM, 2009, S. 265–274 125

[ZH02]   ZUPANCIC, Bernd ; HORZ, Holger: Lecture recording and its use in a traditional university course. In: *ACM SIGCSE Bulletin* Bd. 34 ACM, 2002, S. 24–28 3

[ZHF+05]   ZAHN, Carmen ; HESSE, Friedrich W. ; FINKE, Matthias ; PEA, Roy ; MILLS, Michael ; ROSEN, Joseph: Advanced digital video technologies to support collaborative learning in school education and beyond. In: CHAN, Tak-Wai (Hrsg.): *CSCL*, International Society of the Learning Sciences, 2005, S. 737–742 31, 32

[ZM98]   ZOBEL, Justin ; MOFFAT, Alistair: Exploring the Similarity Space. In: *SIGIR Forum* 32 (1998), Nr. 1, S. 18–34 40

[Zup06]   ZUPANCIC, Bernd: *Vorlesungsaufzeichnungen und digitale Annotationen Einsatz und Nutzen in der Lehre*, Albert-Ludwigs-Universität Freiburg, Dissertation, 2006 30, 31, 32, 122

Appendix A

Source Code

A.1 HTML and Django code rendering the timeline with markers on it

```
1   <div id="markerBar">
2           <div class="timelinebar">
3                   {% for marker in markers %}
4               {% if marker.offset %}
5                   <button type="button" style="left:{{ marker.offset|multiply:100|
                        divide:lecture.duration_sec }}%"
6                       alt="{{marker.marker__name}}" class="markerbutton timeline"
7                       onClick="javascript:seekvideo({{marker.offset}}); $(document)
                        .scrollTop(350)">
8                       <div class="marker" style="background-color:#{{marker.
                        marker__color}}"></div>
9                   </button>
10                  {% elif marker.timestamp %}
11                  <button type="button" style="left:{{ marker.
                        get_live_offset_percentage }}%"
12                      alt="{{marker.marker__name}}" class="markerbutton timeline">
13                      <div class="marker" style="background-color:#{{marker.marker.
                        color}}"></div>
14                  </button>
15              {% endif%}
16              {% endfor %}
17          </div>
18          <div class="timeline">
19              {% num_range 10 as range %}
20                  {% for i in range %}
21                  <div class="circle" style="left:{{ i|multiply:10 }}%"></div>
22                  {% endfor %}
23          </div>
24          <div class="timelinebar">
25              {% num_range 10 as range %}
26                  {% for i in range %}
27                  <a href="">
28                      <div class="number" style="left:{{ i|multiply:10 }}%">
29                          {{lecture.duration_sec|divide:10|multiply:i|divide:60}}
                            min
30                      </div>
```

```
31                    </a>
32                    {% endfor %}
33          </div>
34      </div>
```

A.2 JavaScript code that is responsible for rendering the topic map interface

```
1  function draw_graph(links, keyword)
2  {
3      var vis;
4      var vis = d3.select("body").append("svg:svg").attr("width", width).attr("height",
           height);
5
6      [...]
7
8      // initialize the graph with the nodes
9      var force = d3.layout.force()
10         .nodes(d3.values(nodes))
11         .links(links)
12         .size([width, height])
13         .linkDistance(150)
14         .charge(-300)
15         .start();
16
17     // add labels to the nodes
18     force2 = d3.layout.force()
19         .nodes(labelAnchors)
20         .links(labelAnchorLinks)
21         .size([width, height])
22         .gravity(0)
23         .linkDistance(0)
24         .charge(-100)
25             .start();
26
27     // start the animation
28     force.on("tick", function(d) {tick(d, keyword)})
29
30     // draw the links between the graphs
31     link = vis.selectAll(".link")
32         .data(force.links())
33         .enter().append("line")
34         .attr("class", "link")
35             // change the links width and opacity according to the (normalized)
                   distance between the nodes
36         .style("stroke-opacity", function(d) { return (1.6667*d.value-0.6667); })
37         .style("stroke-width", function(d) { return 10*d.value-4; });
38
39     // add a group to the nodes
40     node = vis.selectAll(".node")
41         .data(force.nodes())
42         .enter().append("g")
43         .attr("class", "node")
44         .call(force.drag);
45
46     // add the node circles
47     node.append("circle")
48         .attr("r", 8)
49         .attr("class", function(d){ if (d.name==keyword) return "start";});
50
51     anchorLink = vis.selectAll("line.anchorLink").data(labelAnchorLinks);
52
53         anchorNode = vis.selectAll("g.anchorNode").data(force2.nodes()).enter().append(
               "svg:g")
```

159

```
54              .attr("class", "anchorNode")
55              .attr("id", function(d, i) { return "b-" + i; });
56
57     anchorNode.append("svg:circle").attr("r", 0).style("fill", "#FFF");
58
59     group = anchorNode.append("svg:g");
60
61         // Put white bar behind text
62         svgrec = group.append("svg:rect");
63         svgrec .transition()
64                 .duration(500)
65                 .attr('width', function(d, i) {return i % 2 == 0 ? 0 : 200})
66                 .attr('height', function(d, i) {return i % 2 == 0 ? 0 : 15})
67                 .attr('x', 0)
68                 .attr('y', -15)
69                 .attr("id", function(d, i) { return "rect-" + i; })
70                 .style('fill', 'url(#grad1)');
71
72         // add label to the nodes
73         svgtext = group.append("svg:text");
74         svgtext.text(function(d, i) {
75             return i % 2 == 0 ? "" : d.node.name;
76         })
77         .attr("class", function(d){
78             if ((d.node.name==keyword)) return "starttext";
79         });
80
81         // add arrow to show icons for further tasks
82         group.append("image")
83             .attr("xlink:href", (function(d, i) {
84                         return i % 2 == 0 ? "" : media_url + "images/buttons/
                                 btn_next_orange.png"
85                     }))
86             .attr("x", -15)
87             .attr("y", -15)
88             .attr("width", 13)
89             .attr("height", 15)
90             .attr("class","imagelink")
91             // when the arrow is clicked add the icons for further tasks underneath the
                 node label
92             .on("click", function(d, i){ return i % 2 == 0 ? "" : add_symbols(this.
                 parentNode.parentNode); });
93     }
94     [...]
```

A.3 Sourcecode that draws the SVG node labels

```
1  <g class="anchorNode" id="b-1" transform="translate
      (616.8647448089914,300.0815341107654)">
2      <circle r="0" style="fill: #ffffff;"></circle>
3      <g>
4          <rect id="rect-1" y="-15" x="0" height="50" width="120" style="fill: #
             grad1;"></rect>
5          <text class="starttext">JavaScript</text>
6          <image xlink:href="/images/buttons/btn_next_orange.png" x="-15" y="-15"
             width="13" height="15" class="imagelink"></image>
7      </g>
8      <a xlink:href="/new_search/?search=JavaScript" target="_blank">
9          <image xlink:href="/images/related_subjects/btn_search_round.png" x="0" y
             ="10" width="24" height="24"></image>
10     </a>
11     <a xlink:href="http://en.wikipedia.org/wiki/JavaScript" target="_blank">
12         <image xlink:href="/images/related_subjects/btn_wikipedia.png" x="30" y="
             10" width="24" height="24" class="imagelink"></image>
13     </a>
14     <a xlink:href="/player/embed/7191/0/?iframe">
15         <image xlink:href="/images/related_subjects/btn_play_round.png" x="60" y=
             "10" width="24" height="24"></image>
16     </a>
17     <image xlink:href="/images/related_subjects/btn_graph.png" x="90" y="10" width=
          "24" height="24" class="imagelink"></image>
18 </g>
```

161

A. SOURCE CODE

Appendix B

Questionnaires

B. QUESTIONNAIRES

B.1 Recruiting Questionnaire for the Laboratory User Test

Empirische Studie zum tele-TASK Portal
Von Franka Grünewald und Haojin Yang
Januar 2013

Rekrutierungs-Fragebogen für den Nutzertest für Indexierungs- und Web 2.0 Funktionen

Name, Vorname: _____

Emailadresse: _____

Alter: _____

Geschlecht: ☐ weiblich ☐ männlich

Wie häufig benutzt Du tele-TASK?

☐ mehrmals in der Woche ☐ ca. 1x in der Woche ☐ mehrmals im Monat

☐ mehrmals im Jahr ☐ nur sporadisch ☐ nie

Hast Du die Vorlesung Informationssicherheit besucht?

☐ ja ☐ nein

Hast Du die tele-TASK Aufzeichnung von Informationssicherheit gesehen?

☐ ja ☐ nein

Wie häufig hast Du bereits die Folienpreview unter dem Videoplayer im tele-TASK Portal benutzt?

☐ mehr als 10x ☐ mehr als 1x ☐ einmal ☐ nie

Wie häufig hast Du bereits das Inhaltsverzeichnis der Vorlesung unter dem Videoplayer im tele-TASK Portal benutzt?

☐ mehr als 10x ☐ mehr als 1x ☐ einmal ☐ nie

Wie häufig hast Du schon die Notizfunktion im tele-TASK Portal genutzt?

☐ mehr als 10x ☐ mehr als 1x ☐ einmal ☐ nie

Falls Du an diesem Test teilnehmen möchtest, würden wir Dich bitten, Dir bis dahin nicht die abgefragten Vorlesungen anzuschauen, die genannten Funktionen zu nutzen oder Dich anderweitig auf den Test vorzubereiten. Das ist nicht notwendig, da Du in dem Test keine Fehler machen kannst. Außerdem würde es die Ergebnisse verfälschen und meinen Test unbrauchbar machen. Vielen Dank.

Seite 1 von 1

B. QUESTIONNAIRES

B.2 User Tasks for the Laboratory User Test of the Annotation Functions

HPI Hasso
Plattner
Institut

Empirische Studie zum tele-TASK Portal
Von Franka Grünewald und Haojin Yang
Januar 2013

Aufgaben für den Nutzertest für Indexierungs- und Web 2.0 Funktionen

Proband Nr.: _____

Aufgabe 1. Bitte suche in einer Vorlesung nach einer vorgegebenen Thematik und finde die Anfangs- und Endzeit im Video heraus:

Runde	Test Video Nr.	Thematik-Anfangszeit	Thematik-Endzeit
1			
2			/
3			
4			
5			

Aufgabe 2. Hier möchten wir Euch bitten, auf den Inhalt der Vorlesungsvideos acht zu geben. Ihr könnt die jeweils angegebenen Hilfsmittel verwenden. Nach dem Videoschauen werden Euch einige Multiple Choice und eine Freitextfrage zu dem gesehenen Thema gestellt.

B. QUESTIONNAIRES

 Hasso
Plattner
Institut

Empirische Studie zum tele-TASK Portal
Von Franka Grünewald und Haojin Yang
Januar 2013

Proband Nr.: _____

Test Video „Kryptoprotokolle"

1. Ein Kryptoprotokoll :
   ist eine Sicherheitsanforderung.
   hat das Ziel des Erreichens von Sicherheit in
   informationsverarbeitenden Prozessen.
   hat das Ziel der erfolgreichen Durchführung der
   Informationsverarbeitung bei Gewährleistung bestimmter
   Sicherheitsanforderungen.
   erzeugt einen Sicherheitsverkehr (Informationskommunikation).

1. Bitte selektiere die richtige(n) Aussage(n):
   Um die Sicherheitsanforderung zur gewährleisten, werden
   kryptografische Methoden benutzt.
   Ein Kryptoprotokoll geht davon aus, dass alle Beteiligten sich
   vertrauen.
   Das Krypotprotokoll basiert darauf, dass alle Beteiligten das Protokoll
   vorschriftsmäßig ausführen.
   An der Kommunikation Beteiligte werden nicht in die Sicherung durch
   das Kryptoprotokoll integriert, d.h. Kommunikationspartner die sich
   gegen einen anderen Kommunikationspartner verschwören, können
   diesen ausspionieren.

2. Wie kann der Bösewicht erkannt werden?
   Beim Abhören eines Kommunikationskanals.
   Beim Manipulieren der abgehörten Daten.
   Beim Berichten der abgehörten Daten.
   Beim Weiterleiten gefälschter Nachrichten.

3. Bitte fasse die Definition vom Kryptoprotokoll in Stichpunkten zusammen.

   _____
   _____
   _____
   _____
   _____
   _____

B.2 User Tasks for the Laboratory User Test of the Annotation Functions

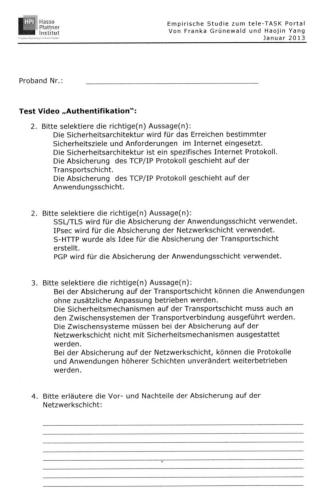

Empirische Studie zum tele-TASK Portal
Von Franka Grünewald und Haojin Yang
Januar 2013

Proband Nr.: _____

Test Video „Authentifikation":

2. Bitte selektiere die richtige(n) Aussage(n):
   Die Sicherheitsarchitektur wird für das Erreichen bestimmter
   Sicherheitsziele und Anforderungen im Internet eingesetzt.
   Die Sicherheitsarchitektur ist ein spezifisches Internet Protokoll.
   Die Absicherung des TCP/IP Protokoll geschieht auf der
   Transportschicht.
   Die Absicherung des TCP/IP Protokoll geschieht auf der
   Anwendungsschicht.

2. Bitte selektiere die richtige(n) Aussage(n):
   SSL/TLS wird für die Absicherung der Anwendungsschicht verwendet.
   IPsec wird für die Absicherung der Netzwerkschicht verwendet.
   S-HTTP wurde als Idee für die Absicherung der Transportschicht
   erstellt.
   PGP wird für die Absicherung der Anwendungsschicht verwendet.

3. Bitte selektiere die richtige(n) Aussage(n):
   Bei der Absicherung auf der Transportschicht können die Anwendungen
   ohne zusätzliche Anpassung betrieben werden.
   Die Sicherheitsmechanismen auf der Transportschicht muss auch an
   den Zwischensystemen der Transportverbindung ausgeführt werden.
   Die Zwischensysteme müssen bei der Absicherung auf der
   Netzwerkschicht nicht mit Sicherheitsmechanismen ausgestattet
   werden.
   Bei der Absicherung auf der Netzwerkschicht, können die Protokolle
   und Anwendungen höherer Schichten unverändert weiterbetrieben
   werden.

4. Bitte erläutere die Vor- und Nachteile der Absicherung auf der
   Netzwerkschicht:

   _____
   _____
   _____
   _____
   _____
   _____
   _____

B. QUESTIONNAIRES

 Hasso
Plattner
Institut

Empirische Studie zum tele-TASK Portal
Von Franka Grünewald und Haojin Yang
Januar 2013

Proband Nr.: _____

Test Video „Zertifikate Server":

1. Ein Zertifikate-Server...
   bietet Web-Services an, um die Zertifikate auszustellen
   ist ein Verzeichnisdienst, der keinen bestimmten Standards unterliegt.
   spielt außerhalb des PKI-Bereichs keine Rolle.
   macht Sperrinformationen über das Netzwerk verfügbar.

2. Bitte selektiere die richtige(n) Aussage(n) über das Directory Service:
   Ein Directory Service ist eine über das Netzwerk verfügbare Datenbank
   mit abrufbaren Daten.
   Die Daten von einem Directory Service sind in Objekte gegliedert und
   alle Objekte sind zwangsläufig einer hierarchischen Struktur
   zugeordnet.
   Die E-Mail-Adresse ist ein Beispielobjekt, das in einem Directory
   Service gespeichert wird.
   Ein Schema wird verwendet, um die Objekte für die Suchfunktion
   bereitzustellen.

3. In einem hierarchisch aufgebauten Directory Services...
   alle Objekte zwingend einem übergeordneten Objekt zugeordnet
   sind Information aller Objekte in einen zentrale Zertifikate-Center
   gespeichert
   gibt es Namenskonventionen, die im Namensraum festgelegt sind.
   folgen die Namen der Objekte bestimmten Regeln, die Teil eines
   Schemas sind.

4. Bitte beschreibe kurz die wichtigsten Prinzipien der PKI (Public Key
   Infrastruktur).
   _____
   _____
   _____
   _____
   _____
   _____
   _____

B.3 Results of the User Tasks for the Laboratory User Test of the Annotation Functions

 Hasso
Plattner
Institut

Empirische Studie zum tele-TASK Portal
Von Franka Grünewald und Haojin Yang
Januar 2013

Videomaterial und Lösungen für den Nutzertest
für Indexierungs- und Web 2.0 Funktionen –
Aufgabe 1

Aufgabe 1.

	URL	Thema	Start	Ende	Länge
test video 1:	http://www5-dev.hpi.uni-potsdam.de/archive/video/flash/13784/	Schlüsselverteilun g mit KAS nach diffie-Hellman	0:43:46	1:00:43	16 mins 57s
test video 2:	http://www5-dev.hpi.uni-potsdam.de/archive/video/flash/13878/	Trust Center und seine Komponenten	0:25:46	0:37:46	12mins 0s
test video 3:	http://www5-dev.hpi.uni-potsdam.de/archive/video/flash/13814/	Station-to-Station Protokoll	0:26:51	0:38:51	12mins 2s
test video 4:	http://www5-dev.hpi.uni-potsdam.de/archive/video/flash/12980/	Deterministische Primzahltests	0:03:52	0:20:44	16mins 52s
test video 5:	http://www5-dev.hpi.uni-potsdam.de/archive/video/flash/13110/	Substitutions-Chiffern	0:03:59	0:18:17	14mins 18s

Aufgabe 2.

	URL	Thema	Start	Ende	Länge
test video clip 1:	http://www5-dev.hpi.uni-potsdam.de/archive/video/flash/12759/461	Kryptoprotokoll-Definition	0:07:41	0:16:32	8mins 51s
test video clip 2:	http://www5-dev.hpi.uni-potsdam.de/archive/video/flash/13686/1231	TCP/IP Sicherheitsarchite kturen	0:20:31	0:29:50	9mins 19s
test video clip 3:	http://www5-dev.hpi.uni-potsdam.de/archive/video/flash/14053/0	Zertifikate Server' Einführung + Directory Services	0:00:20	0:09:55	9mins 35s

172

Hasso
Plattner
Institut

Empirische Studie zum tele-TASK Portal
Von Franka Grünewald und Haojin Yang
Januar 2013

Lösungen für den Nutzertest für Indexierungs- und Web 2.0 Funktionen – Aufgabe 2

Test Video „Kryptoprotokolle"

1. Ein Kryptoprotokoll :
   ist eine Sicherheitsanforderung.
   hat das Ziel des Erreichens von Sicherheit in informationsverarbeitenden Prozessen.
   hat das Ziel der erfolgreichen Durchführung der Informationsverarbeitung bei Gewährleistung bestimmter Sicherheitsanforderungen.
   erzeugt einen Sicherheitsverkehr (Informationskommunikation).

2. Bitte wähle die richtige Aussage aus.
   Um die Sicherheitsanforderung zur gewährleisten, werden kryptografische Methoden benutzt.
   Ein Kryptoprotokoll geht davon aus, dass alle Beteiligten sich vertrauen.
   Das Kryptoprotokoll basiert darauf, dass alle Beteiligten das Protokoll vorschriftsmäßig ausführen.
   An der Kommunikation Beteiligte werden nicht in die Sicherung durch das Kryptoprotokoll integriert, d.h. Kommunikationspartner die sich gegen einen anderen Kommunikationspartner verschwören, können diesen ausspionieren.

3. Wie kann der Bösewicht erkannt werden?
   Beim Abhören eines Kommunikationskanals.
   Beim Manipulieren der abgehörten Daten.
   Beim Berichten der abgehörten Daten.
   Beim Weiterleiten gefälschter Nachrichten.

4. Bitte fasse die Definition vom Kryptoprotokoll in Stichpunkten zusammen.
   a. Fest vorgegebene folge von Schritten mit jeweils genau spezifizierten Aktionen
   b. Beteiligte müssen es ausführen
   c. Verteilter informationsverarbeitender Prozess soll mit vorgegebenen Sicherheitsanforderungen erfolgreich durchgeführt werden

Test Video „Authentifikation":

1. Bitte selektiere die richtige(n) Aussage(n):
   Die Sicherheitsarchitektur wird für das Erreichen bestimmter Sicherheitsziele und Anforderungen im Internet eingesetzt.
   Die Sicherheitsarchitektur ist eine spezifisches Internet Protokoll.
   Die Absicherung des TCP/IP Protokoll geschieht auf der Transportschicht.
   Die Absicherung des TCP/IP Protokoll geschieht auf der Anwendungsschicht erfolgen.

2. Bitte selektiere die richtige(n) Aussage(n):
   SSL/TLS wird für die Absicherung der Anwendungsschicht verwendet.
   IPsec wird für die Absicherung der Netzwerkschicht verwendet.
   S-HTTP wurde als Idee für die Absicherung der Transportschicht erstellt.
   PGP wird für die Absicherung der Anwendungsschicht verwendet.

B. QUESTIONNAIRES

 Hasso
Plattner
Institut

Empirische Studie zum tele-TASK Portal
Von Franka Grünewald und Haojin Yang
Januar 2013

3. Bitte selektiere die richtige(n) Aussage(n):
**Bei der Absicherung auf der Transportschicht können die
Anwendungen ohne zusätzliche Anpassung betrieben werden.**
Die Sicherheitsmechanismen auf der Transportschicht muss auch an den
Zwischensystemen der Transportverbindung ausgeführt werden.
Die Zwischensysteme müssen bei der Absicherung auf der Netzwerkschicht
nicht mit Sicherheitsmechanismen ausgestattet werden.
**Bei der Absicherung auf der Netzwerkschicht, können die Protokolle
und Anwendungen höherer Schichten unverändert weiterbetrieben
werden.**

4. Bitte erläutere die Vor- und Nachteile der Absicherung auf der Netzwerkschicht:
   a. Alle Protokolle und Anwendungen höherer Schichten können unverändert
   weiterbetrieben werden.
   b. Absicherung aufwendig, da Zwischensysteme mit aktiven Schutzmechanismen
   ausgestattet werden müssen.
   c. Spezifischen Anforderungen des Anwenders kann nur allgemein entsprochen
   werden.

Test Video „Zertifikate Server":

1. Ein Zertifikate-Server...
   bietet Web-Services an, um die Zertifikate auszustellen
   ist ein Verzeichnisdienst, der keinen bestimmten Standards unterliegt.
   spielt außerhalb des PKI-Bereichs keine Rolle.
   macht Sperrinformationen über das Netzwerk verfügbar.

2. Bitte selektiere die richtige(n) Aussage(n) über das Directory Service:
   **Ein Directory Service ist eine über das Netzwerk verfügbare
   Datenbank mit abrufbaren Daten.**
   Die Daten von einem Directory Service sind in Objekte gegliedert und alle
   Objekte sind zwangsläufig einer hierarchischen Struktur zugeordnet.
   Die E-Mail-Adresse ist ein Beispielobjekt, das in einem Directory Service
   gespeichert wird.
   Ein Schema wird verwendet, um die Objekte für die Suchfunktion
   bereitzustellen.

3. In einem hierarchisch aufgebauten Directory Services...
   alle Objekte zwingend einem übergeordneten Objekt zugeordnet
   sind Information aller Objekte in einen zentrale Zertifikate-Center gespeichert
   gibt es Namenskonventionen, die im Namensraum festgelegt sind.
   **folgen die Namen der Objekte bestimmten Regeln, die Teil eines
   Schemas sind.**

4. Bitte beschreibe kurz die wichtigsten Prinzipien der PKI (Public Key Infrastruktur).

   a. Beglaubigung der Bindung eines öffentlichen Schlüssels an einen Nutzer
   b. Zertifikate werden vom Trust Center ausgestellt, um diese Beglaubigung zu
   erstellen.
   c. Zertifikate und Sperrinformationen werden über das Netzwerk verfügbar
   gemacht.

B.4 Post Test Questionnaire for the Laboratory User Test of the Annotation Functions

Hasso
Plattner
Institut

Empirische Studie zum tele-TASK Portal
Von Franka Grünewald und Haojin Yang
Januar 2013

Post-Test-Fragebogen für das tele-TASK Portal

Name, Vorname: _____

Wie bewertest Du die einzelnen Indexierungs- und Annotations-Tools?

Folienpreview	☐	☐	☐	☐	☐		☐
Inhaltsverzeichnis	☐	☐	☐	☐	☐		☐
Keywords	☐	☐	☐	☐	☐		☐
Digitale Mitschrift	☐	☐	☐	☐	☐		☐
Marker	☐	☐	☐	☐	☐		☐
	Nicht sinnvoll				Sehr sinnvoll		nicht genutzt

Die Verwendung der folgenden tele-TASK Funktionen wird mir dabei helfen, Vorlesungen zukünftig schneller online anzuschauen.

Inhaltsverzeichnis	☐	☐	☐	☐	☐		☐
Digitale Mitschrift	☐	☐	☐	☐	☐		☐
Folienpreview	☐	☐	☐	☐	☐		☐
Marker	☐	☐	☐	☐	☐		☐
Keywords	☐	☐	☐	☐	☐		☐
	Stimme zu				Stimme nicht zu		nicht genutzt

Die folgenden tele-TASK Funktionen waren einfach in der Benutzung.

Digitale Mitschrift	☐	☐	☐	☐	☐		☐
Keywords	☐	☐	☐	☐	☐		☐
Marker	☐	☐	☐	☐	☐		☐
Folienpreview	☐	☐	☐	☐	☐		☐
Inhaltsverzeichnis	☐	☐	☐	☐	☐		☐
	Stimme zu				Stimme nicht zu		nicht genutzt

Seite 1 von 3

HPI Hasso Plattner Institut

Empirische Studie zum tele-TASK Portal
Von Franka Grünewald und Haojin Yang
Januar 2013

Die Verwendung der folgenden tele-TASK Funktionen war zu langsam.

Keywords	☐	☐	☐	☐	☐		☐
Marker	☐	☐	☐	☐	☐		☐
Folienpreview	☐	☐	☐	☐	☐		☐
Inhaltsverzeichnis	☐	☐	☐	☐	☐		☐
Digitale Mitschrift	☐	☐	☐	☐	☐		☐

Stimme zu   Stimme nicht zu   nicht genutzt

Die Verwendung der folgenden tele-TASK Funktionen hat Spaß gemacht.

Inhaltsverzeichnis	☐	☐	☐	☐	☐		☐
Digitale Mitschrift	☐	☐	☐	☐	☐		☐
Folienpreview	☐	☐	☐	☐	☐		☐
Marker	☐	☐	☐	☐	☐		☐
Keywords	☐	☐	☐	☐	☐		☐

Stimme zu   Stimme nicht zu   nicht genutzt

Was sind Deiner Meinung nach die größten Vor- und Nachteile der Indexierungsfunktionen (Inhaltsverzeichnis, Folienpreview, Keywords)?

Vorteile	Nachteile

B. QUESTIONNAIRES

Empirische Studie zum tele-TASK Portal
Von Franka Grünewald und Haojin Yang
Januar 2013

Was sind Deiner Meinung nach die größten Vor- und Nachteile der Annotationsfunktionen (Mitschrift und Marker)?

Vorteile	Nachteile

Was hat an den ausprobierten tele-TASK Funktionalitäten für Dich gar nicht funktioniert? Warum?

Welche der ausprobierten tele-TASK Funktionalitäten war für Dich am nützlichsten? Warum?

Hast Du Funktionen im Zusammenhang mit dem Videoplayer vermisst? Welche?

Möchtest Du uns noch etwas anderes mitteilen? Wir sind für jedes Feedback dankbar!

B.5 Questionnaire for the User Test of the Manuscript Function in a Seminar Setting

Fragebogen für Manuskript-Funktion des tele-TASK-Portals

1. Geschlecht   Männlich   Weiblich

2. Altersgruppe   Unter 18   18 – 24   24 – 30   Über 30

3. Wie häufig hast Du...

	täglich	einige Male pro Woche	einmal pro Woche	einige Male im Monat	seltener
a. ... Deinen Laptop im Studium bisher benutzt?					
b. ... bisher im Studium auf Stift und Zettel mitgeschrieben?					
c. ... bereits Notizen während der Vorlesung oder dem Seminar auf dem Laptop geschrieben?					
d. ... bis jetzt Vorlesungsaufzeichnungen verwendet?					

4. Wie häufig hast Du bisher Videos annotiert?
   über 50 x   ca. 20 x   ca. 10 x   zwischen 6-10 x   zwischen 1-5 x   1x   noch nie

5. Wie zufrieden warst Du mit dem digitalen Mitschreiben im tele-TASK Portal!?
   Sehr zufrieden   Gar nicht zufrieden

6. Wie zufrieden warst Du mit dem Mitschreiben auf Zettel und Stift?
   Gar nicht zufrieden   Sehr zufrieden

7. Welche Art der Mitschrift gefällt Dir tendenziell besser?
   Stift & Papier   Digitale Mitschrift

8. Welche Methode hat mehr Spaß gemacht?
   Stift & Papier   Digitale Mitschrift

9. Welche Methode war schneller?
   Stift & Papier   Digitale Mitschrift

10. Bitte bewerte die folgenden Aussagen zur Mitschrift-Funktion.

	Stimme voll zu	Stimme eher zu	Weder noch	Stimme eher nicht zu	Stimme gar nicht zu
a. Die Funktion der digitalen Mitschrift gefällt mir.					
b. Mit der digitalen Mitschrift habe ich mehr mitgeschrieben als sonst.					
c. Ich hatte Probleme, die Funktion der digitalen Mitschriften zu nutzen.					
d. Das Mitschreiben mit dem Tool hat mich vom Vortrag abgelenkt.					
e. Ich finde es sinnvoll, die Zeitmarken der Mitschriften zu nutzen, um bestimmte Stellen im Video wieder zu finden.					
f. Die Durchsuchbarkeit der digitalen Mitschriften ist kein Vorteil der digitalen Notizen im Vergleich zu Mitschriften mit Zettel und Stift.					
g. Die digitalen Mitschriften ausdrucken zu können ist eine Funktionalität, die ich nicht hilfreich finde.					
h. Digitale Mitschriften parallel zu einer live stattfindenden Vorlesung machen zu können finde ich wichtig.					
i. Digitale Mitschriften parallel zu einer im Portal abrufbaren Vorlesung machen zu können finde ich wichtig.					
j. Die Möglichkeit, die Mitschriften in einer Lerngruppe gemeinsam erstellen zu können finde ich sinnvoll.					

11. Wenn für Dich die Mitschrift-Funktion in einer Lerngruppe nicht oder wenig sinnvoll ist, warum? (Mehrfachantwort möglich)

Mit Vorlesungsvideos arbeite ich nicht.

Ich arbeite lieber allein.

Ich mache eh immer mehr als andere.

Ich hatte Schwierigkeiten bei der Benutzung des Web-Interface.

Gruppenarbeit liegt mir nicht.

Ich finde die Funktion an sich nicht sinnvoll.

Sonstiges: _____

12. Wenn für Dich die Mitschrift-Funktion in einer Lerngruppe sinnvoll ist, was gefällt Dir besonders?
(Mehrfachantwort möglich)

Die aktive Mitarbeit.

Hinterher habe ich eine gute Zusammenfassung.

Gruppenarbeit macht mir Spaß.

Ich schreibe sowieso mit und eine digitale Mitschrift
ist attraktiv.

In der Gruppe muss ich nicht ganz so viel machen.

Ich kann damit sehen, was die anderen wichtig finden.

Sonstiges: _____

13. Wie viel hast Du im Vergleich zu Deinen Teamkollegen mitgeschrieben.

Sehr viel mehr   Mehr   Ausgewogen   Weniger   Viel weniger

14. Was findest Du besonders gut an der Mitschrift-Funktion?

_____
_____
_____

15. Was gefällt Dir an der Mitschrift-Funktion besonders wenig?

_____
_____
_____

16. Welche Verbesserungswünsche hast Du für die Mitschrift-Funktion?

_____
_____
_____
_____

B.6 Questionnaire for the Expert Evaluation of the Topic Map Data

Studie Semantische Topic Map - Expertenevaluation

Topic Map: *{Algorithm} {Keyword}*					
Bitte ordne die Topic Map für die Klassifizierung zu.					
Das Thema der Topic Map ist global	☐	☐	☐	☐	☐ Das Thema der Topic Map ist detailliert
Wie findest Du die Auswahl an Themen und Beziehungen, bezogen auf das ausgewählte Stichwort? – für Topic Map					
Enthält falsche Werte	☐	☐	☐	☐	☐ Enthält keine Falschen Werte
Ist umfangreich genug	☐	☐	☐	☐	☐ Es fehlen Daten
Ist zu feingranular	☐	☐	☐	☐	☐ Ist zu umfangreich
Die Auswahl ist sinnvoll	☐	☐	☐	☐	☐ Die Auswahl ist nicht sinnvoll
Gibt einen sinnvollen Überblick über das Thema	☐	☐	☐	☐	☐ Gibt keinen sinnvollen Überblick über das Thema

B.7 Questionnaire for the User Evaluation of the Semantic Topic Map Function in a Pre-Study

Pre-Study Semantic Topic Map Prototype

Gender: ☐ female   ☐ male

Age:

Field of study/studies:

What was your first impression of the semantic topic map?

_____

_____

I would use the semantic topic map in a learning context to...

_____

_____

I consider the semantic topic map...

very helpful   ☐ ☐ ☐ ☐ ☐   not helpful at all

very intuitive to use ☐ ☐ ☐ ☐ ☐   not intuitive at all

I think it is very useful to combine the semantic topic map with personal lecture video annotations.

Yes, totally   ☐ ☐ ☐ ☐ ☐   No, not at all

I see the advantages of the semantic topic map in...

_____

_____

I see the disadvantages of the semantic topic map in...

_____

_____

B.7 Questionnaire for the User Evaluation of the Semantic Topic Map Function

B.8 Questionnaire for the User Evaluation of the Semantic Topic Map Function in the Main Study

Studie Semantische Topic Map & Manuscript

Geschlecht: ☐ weiblich   ☐ männlich

Alter:

Studienfach:

Was war Dein erster Eindruck von der semantischen Topic Map?

_____

_____

Im Lernkontext würde ich die semantische Topic Map nutzen, um…

_____

_____

Ich finde die semantische Topic Map …

| Sehr hilfreich | ☐ | ☐ | ☐ | ☐ | ☐ | Gar nicht hilfreich |
| Sehr intuitiv zu nutzen | ☐ | ☐ | ☐ | ☐ | ☐ | Gar nicht intuitiv |

Ich finde es sinnvoll, die semantische Topic Map mit persönlichen Vorlesungsvideo-Annotationen zu verbinden.

| Ja, auf jeden Fall | ☐ | ☐ | ☐ | ☐ | ☐ | Nein, überhaupt nicht |

Ich sehe die Vorteile der semantischen Topic Map in…

_____

_____

Ich sehe die Nachteile der semantischen Topic Map in…

_____

_____

B.8 Questionnaire for the User Evaluation of the Semantic Topic Map Function

Ich konnte mit der semantischen Topic Map leichter erkennen, welche Themen für das Themengebiet, das ich gerade lerne, noch relevant sind.

Nein, überhaupt nicht   ☐ ☐ ☐ ☐ ☐   Ja, auf jeden Fall

Durch die semantische Topic Map direkt auf verwandte Videos zu verweisen ist hilfreich.

Ja, auf jeden Fall   ☐ ☐ ☐ ☐ ☐   Nein, überhaupt nicht

Es ist sehr hilfreich durch die Topic Map auf verwandte Schlüsselwörter zu navigieren.

Ja, auf jeden Fall   ☐ ☐ ☐ ☐ ☐   Nein, überhaupt nicht

Über die semantische Topic Map direkt zur Suchfunktion zu navigieren ist sehr nützlich.

Nein, überhaupt nicht   ☐ ☐ ☐ ☐ ☐   Ja, auf jeden Fall

Die semantische Topic Map hat mir einen guten Überblick über das Themengebiet gegeben.

Nein, überhaupt nicht   ☐ ☐ ☐ ☐ ☐   Ja, auf jeden Fall

Noch ein paar Fragen zur Annotationsfunktion

Ich würde die Manuscript-Funktion häufiger nutzen, wenn es im Gruppenmodus ein Newsfeed mit aktuellen Gruppenbeiträgen gibt.

Ja, auf jeden Fall   ☐ ☐ ☐ ☐ ☐   Nein, überhaupt nicht

Ich wäre motivierter die Manuscript-Funktion zu nutzen, wenn sie wie ein Wiki funktionierte (mit allen Formatierungen, Bearbeitungsoption für alle Gruppenmitglieder und einer History).

Ja, auf jeden Fall   ☐ ☐ ☐ ☐ ☐   Nein, überhaupt nicht

Eine Statistik über die Beteiligung der Gruppenmitglieder an dem Schreiben von Annotationen in der Manuscript-Funktion erhöht meine Motivation.

Nein, überhaupt nicht   ☐ ☐ ☐ ☐ ☐   Ja, auf jeden Fall

B. QUESTIONNAIRES

B.9   Questionnaire for the User Evaluation in a MOOC Scenario

openHPI User Survey 2013

0% [_____] 100%

[English ⬦]

Evaluation of User Interaction Possibilities with E-Lectures

A semantic topic map visualizes different keywords and their connections. The strength of these connections is shown via the opacity and thickness of the connecting lines.

Please evaluate different aspects of the semantic topic map with the help of the following questions.

	very much	rather much	neutral	less	not at all	No answer
How much are you interested in finding your own learning path through the learning material provided in the platform and thus work independent of the course layout?	○	○	○	○	○	⊙
How helpful do you think is the visualization of topics and their connection in a topic map for you?	○	○	○	○	○	⊙
How helpful do you think is it to see related topics in the topic map that are not actually part of the course?	○	○	○	○	○	⊙
How often would you use such a topic map?	○	○	○	○	○	⊙

191

B. QUESTIONNAIRES

A user-generated annotation allows you to create lecture notes at a specific point within the video. Afterwards you receive a manuscript with timestamps that allow you to jump into the video at the point in time when the annotation was created. Please evaluate this function according to the following questions.

	yes, totally	rather yes	neutral	rather no	not at all	No answer
I would be motivated to use a function to write a digital manuscript that can be shared and edited in a learning group.	○	○	○	○	○	⊙
I would be more motivated to use a video annotation function when it worked like a wiki (with formatting and editing options for group members as well as a history).	○	○	○	○	○	⊙

I would be more motivated to use a digital manuscript writing function in a learning group...

	yes, totally	rather yes	neutral	rather no	not at all	No answer
...if a newsfeed with the latest contributions existed.	○	○	○	○	○	⊙
...if a statistic of the indivdual group member's participation would be visible.	○	○	○	○	○	⊙
...if participation would be rewarded with bonus points or badges.	○	○	○	○	○	⊙

192